Memories
of
Caithness

compiled by
Christopher J. Uncles

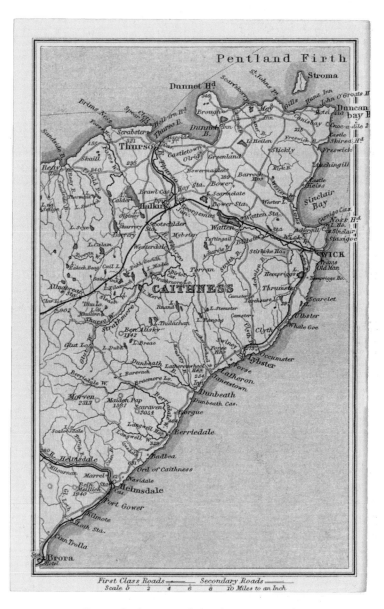

Stenlake Publishing Ltd.
2004

FOREWORD

Thomas Pennant was not only a naturalist, antiquary and observant traveller, but also a gifted writer whose works included three volumes of *Tours in Scotland*, published in 1790. Twenty-one years prior to their publication he had penetrated the remote and little-known region of Caithness, which he noted was 'little better than an immense morass, with here and there some fruitful spots of oats and bere [a type of barley], and much coarse grass, almost all wild there being as yet very little cultivated'.

Pennant's observations preceded a century of progress that saw a number of key and far-reaching improvements which would promote general economic growth in Caithness, and for many, change life for the better. The building of new roads and the coming of the railway provided improved access to a region previously highly dependent on sea transport, while the encouragement of good husbandry and the development of planned communities and small harbours to exploit fishing activities – especially the herring and curing industries – all boosted economic activity and employment. The names of some of the 'improvers' who were responsible for what was a giant leap forward from Pennant's day appear in the following pages.

Although the great wealth generated from the once all-important herring fishing industry proved transitory and has now vanished, much remains that is permanent. Traditionally employment has been sustained by the three 'Fs' – farming (including stock rearing), fishing and flagstones – and today these staples are augmented by tourism, regarded as increasingly important. There have been some landmark developments since the Second World War: Caithness Glass, established in 1961, was the first new glass-making factory to be built in Scotland in the twentieth century, while at Dounreay the United Kingdom Atomic Energy Authority's plant has become the county's single biggest employer and the main plank of the local economy.

As the title suggests, *Memories of Caithness* is concerned with the past, and is illustrated with postcards and photographs from my own collection dating from the 1860s to about 1950. The illustrations follow an anticlockwise route commencing at the Ord of Caithness, and are arranged in two broad sequences – the North Sea Coast and the Pentland Coast – with each section having diversions inland. 'Deepest Caithness', my name for the Flow Country, is featured in the latter. An introduction provides a general background, while a following section gives some biographical details of some of the all-important men whose work is featured, the photographers, through whose eyes (and lenses) we can gain a better understanding of the past.

Christopher J. Uncles

© Christopher J. Uncles 2004
First published in the United Kingdom, 2004,
by Stenlake Publishing Ltd.
Telephone: 01290 551122
Printed by Cordfall Ltd., Glasgow, G21 2QA

ISBN 1 84033 298 0

In the meeting- or ceilidh-houses at night nothing was talked about but the coming fishing. 'Creels of silver herring will turn into creels of silver crowns' became the joke that never lost its gleam.

The Silver Darlings, Neil M. Gunn, 1941

INTRODUCTION

Over aeons of time our landscape has been moulded by enormous and quite differing forces on a scale difficult to comprehend: volcanic activity, intense heat and cold, the gouging and grinding of huge ice sheets on the move, and by the pounding action of wind-driven seas on our coasts – processes that are continuous and unending. About 350 million years ago most of Caithness, together with Orkney, was covered by a vast inland sea known as Lake Orcadie. This lake was fed by rivers and streams which over time transported rock debris, silt and soil, laying down the layers of bedrock seen with such striking effect in Caithness cliff and coastal features. Towards the end of the last Ice Age, movements made by receding, melting glaciers deposited rich alluvial and morainic material across the county, shaping and enriching the undulating landscape familiar today. Millennia later, the fossils of corals, shells and fish entombed in the Old Red Sandstone beds in what was once Lake Orcadie await the tap of the geologist's hammer to see the light of day once again.

In much the same way that Pembrokeshire is sometimes referred to as 'Little England beyond Wales', so Caithness has often been described as the 'Lowlands beyond the Highlands'. How apt, for this is a lowland county with physical characteristics which are quite different from those of neighbouring Sutherland. The few mountains of modest size, known collectively as the 'Heights of Caithness' (everything is relative), lie in the south-east on the border with Sutherland. They are visible from afar over an almost featureless landscape where vistas lead the eye in turn over immense tracts of blanket bog (the Flow Country), low hills and fertile farmland dotted with neat farmsteads, sheep and cattle, or across the glittering sea of the Pentland Firth to Orkney. Castles and defensive fortifications ring the perimeter of the spectacular and often dramatic coastline, which has a fine variety of natural formations: cliffs, caves, arches, isolated pillars and rock bridges. Bold headlands erupt at the Ord of Caithness, Noss, Duncansby, Dunnet and Holborn, providing observation points for the teeming bird life along the cliffs. In this highly individual county one is never more than a few miles from the sea, and everywhere the skyscapes are truly Olympian.

While John O' Groats is both a name and a location familiar to millions, I suspect that little is generally known about this triangular-shaped county occupying the extreme north-east of mainland Britain. Bounded to the north by the Pentland Firth and by the North Sea to the east, and consisting of about 440,000 acres of bare moorland, lochs and hills, these northern lands face towards Norway, with whom they shared much history between the eighth and thirteenth centuries. Even further back in time, Stone Age people and Picts left their imprint on the landscape by way of a wealth of brochs, hut circles, cairns, souterrains, wags (enclosures unique to Caithness) and standing stones. The waters of the 'Stormy Pentland' were familiar to Phoenician trading vessels and to the Romans. Later, the occupying Vikings (also sometimes known as Northmen or Creekmen), who were both raiders and traders, exploited the natural resources that made Caithness the 'granary of Norway'; evidence of their settlement in this northern redoubt survives in the many place-names of Norse origin that remain to this day.

Since ancient times men have quarried and worked the plentiful supply of naturally occurring stone, a valuable and durable local resource. That the men of Caithness have had a natural affinity with – and understanding of – working in stone throughout history cannot be doubted, for the evidence is to be seen everywhere. One cannot but admire the skills of those who built, for example, the Grey Cairns of Camster about 3000 BC, and marvel that these cairns were made by a people possessing none of the advantages of modern tools. Closer to our own times, many vernacular buildings and small harbours in Caithness have been beautifully engineered and constructed, and there are also some fine public buildings made of local stone in Thurso and Wick. Although conducted on a much smaller scale than previously, such work continues in the county's flagstone industry where high quality stone is still extracted for paving. At one time vast quantities were quarried not only for use as flagstones, but also for walls and roofing, and exported all over the world. Flagstone field dykes are commonly seen across the county; slabs stood on end as boundary markers make a distinctive impact on the landscape.

Important as the growing of crops, raising of cattle and quarrying have been (and continue to be), the fact remains that for more than a century the prosperity of Caithness largely depended on fishing, especially for herring (the 'silver darlings'). As the herring fishery forms a continuing theme throughout the book, further comment can be found accompanying the illustrations themselves. Suffice to say that fishing for herring no longer pays the wages. The great days of enormous catches are long gone, as is Wick's reputation as 'Herringopolis', the largest herring port in the world.

Population trends have moved in line with highly varying degrees of economic fortune. In 1801 the population of the county was recorded at 22,609, rising to 41,111 at the height of the herring boom in 1861. This figure declined during the late nineteenth century and stood at 33,870 in 1901. Further decline to 28,285 (1921) was seen following the First World War, with a continuing downward spiral to 25,656 ten years later.

SOME NOTABLE CAITHNESS PHOTOGRAPHERS

Prior to the latter decades of the twentieth century, by far the largest amount of photographic work represented on postcards was undertaken by photographers whose names went unrecorded, with the result that they remain quite anonymous. Another regrettable fact is that many archives – the lifeblood of any photographer's work – have been lost, fatally damaged or even deliberately destroyed by individuals having no appreciation of their worth as historical resources. Whilst researching this series of books I have become aware of some catastrophic losses of Highland photographic history. For the most part these took place many years ago, and the hope must be that today as a nation we are better educated and informed about the significance of such material and the place of the photograph in local and national history. Readers of my previous books will know that whenever possible I have tried to remedy the anonymity of postcard photographers by either devoting a few words to a particular photographer, drawing attention to his work where details could be discovered, or, as in the case of *Oban and the Land of Lorn*, by providing a major profile of one whose life's work has been sadly lost to us.

Several highly skilled and dedicated Caithness photographers, some of whose work is shown here, were responsible for capturing a huge number of notable scenes from the past on camera, and it is to them that I wish to devote the second part of this introduction. The first photographic life to be portrayed is that of a man who was taking pictures soon after the birth of photography. Fortunately, matters concerning the survival of his own extensive archive were resolved most satisfactorily, albeit only in 1975, nearly 80 years after his death. During the last week of June 1896, the *Northern Ensign* and the *John O' Groat Journal* reported that a local man who had travelled to Edinburgh seeking specialist medical advice and treatment had unexpectedly died there; both newspapers carried fulsome tributes. While he may have been virtually unknown in Auld Reekie, except perhaps in photographic circles, in his home town of Wick he was a household name. He was **Alexander Johnston**, photographer and artist. The *Journal* continued:

The second son of the late Mr W. Johnston, plumber, Mr Johnston was born in Wick in 1838, and had thus reached the age of 58 years. In his boyhood he evinced a strong interest in art studies, and gave special attention to photography, a practical knowledge of which he acquired with scarcely any assistance. His first studio was at his father's house at Willowbank, and in a short time he became noted as an expert and skilful photographer. The work which he produced not only compared favourably with but excelled much that came from the hands of those who were much older and had more experience than himself; and in a short time he stood at the top of his profession. A good many years ago he was joined as a partner by his brother, Mr James Johnston, who has now attained to almost equal eminence in the profession. The brothers carried out an extensive business together in the well-known rooms in Brims' Buildings, Bridge Street, until they removed about two years ago to their handsome and commodious new premises in the Market Place; and a branch establishment was opened a year or two ago in Thurso.

Naturally, studio portraiture formed a significant aspect of his business, and there will be many who still have a Johnston picture of themselves taken as children tucked away in the family photograph album at home. But he was never studio-bound and many of his masterpieces were taken in Wick, especially around the harbour where the frenetic activity provided a multitude of superb opportunities for a photographer eager to capture such scenes on the unwieldy photographic glass plates then in use. In other ways he was a pioneer, mastering as he did a process for combining a number of negatives so that the whole could be printed as one picture. During the famous, but short-lived, Sutherland gold rush of 1869 he transported his camera equipment in a horse-drawn caravan to photograph the hopefuls panning for gold at Kildonan, a return journey which took eight days. The resultant pictures show the only recorded stampede for gold in our islands. He was a frequent contributor to various photographic journals, and was honoured by his admission as a Fellow of the Royal Photographic Society.

William Johnston succeeded his late father and uncle, the business in Wick (with the branch at Thurso) becoming his sole responsibility from 1908. His proprietorship witnessed many advances in photography including the introduction of roll film and the Kodak Box Brownie camera, which made the hobby widely available to all. Like other studios of his day, he undertook the processing of film for individuals and local chemists, while at the same time continuing to photograph almost everything that moved – and much that did not! – around the county's two most populous centres. In this work he was joined from 1932 by his son **Alexander Johnston**, who travelled daily to Thurso by train to oversee the work of that branch until changing circumstances resulted in the closure of the business there in 1938. The Second World War intervened, after which Alexander returned to the family firm to re-establish the threads of his life in Civvy Street. His father, William, died in 1950, but the Johnston Studio continued in Alexander's hands until his own retirement in 1974. Three generations of the same family spanning 115 years of photography must surely be something of a record. Over this period about 100,000 photographs were produced.

However, at this crucial stage, circumstances could so easily have turned into one of those tragedies of loss I referred to earlier. Fortunately, two far-sighted people – Alexander Johnston and Iain Sutherland – ensured that the whole collection, which dated back in time to the 1860s, was moved into the protection and care of the then recently formed Wick Society. Large numbers of glass plate negatives were involved – some full-, some half- and others quarter-plate. Many had congealed together, others were cracked, while yet more had suffered poor storage or handling with the result that numerous images were beyond saving. Nevertheless, a lengthy programme of work undertaken by volunteer members of the Wick Society ensured the survival of some 45,000 plates and large numbers of film negatives which are now stored at the Heritage Centre in Bank Row, a priceless treasure-trove of days past.

Next on the photographic scene is **John Gemmell Humphrey**, who was born in Kilmarnock on 30 December 1868. His early life was blighted by sadness: he never knew his mother, who died two weeks after his birth, and although his father subsequently remarried, his stepmother died when he was only twelve years old. Just eight years later in 1889 his father, too, passed on due to alcoholism; he was aged only 49. Mr Humphrey Snr. had successfully established a photographic studio in King Street, Kilmarnock, and John gained some early training there, which was further consolidated for a short time with experience at a large firm in Glasgow.

The exact circumstances which took him north to Wick about 1889 are not known, but maybe life in Ayrshire held too many unhappy memories for him and he sought a complete break. Whatever the reasons, that year found him employed at Mr P. Swanson's photographic studio at 4 River Street and, two years later following Swanson's death, Humphrey took over the premises on his own account. In the 1891 census he is listed both as photographic artist and employer. Thus, at the age of 22 and after suffering many setbacks in his young life, he had his own studio and the rest of his life before him. One can only speculate whether he ever entertained any doubts about his new venture. After all, he was an incomer and the Johnston Studio, then just across the river in Bridge Street, was already very well-established. Could he make a satisfactory living and would there be enough business for two such studios in this small town in the farthest corner of mainland Britain?

In fact, he was to conduct his business from River Street with success for over 50 years. His output was prodigious and he photographed landscapes and buildings, special events and social occasions plus, of course, the periodic Wick processions and parades. He also undertook studio portraiture and was interested in new developments such as cinephotography, making a 9 mm film of Wick Harbour in 1907. Sadly the whereabouts of this film are not now known. His work occasionally took him into neighbouring Sutherland, and the most distant photograph I have of his was taken at the Tongue Hotel. He was an excellent photographer, and that is an opinion of one of his distinguished peers in Wick who knew him. No one could doubt the quality of his work or that he possessed a natural eye for artistic composition, something that is so often evidenced in his photographs. According to information shown me, his grandson (also John), who resides in Canada, believes

Humphrey retired in May 1938, although the valuation rolls indicate that the River Street studio remained in his name for a further five years. John Gemmell Humphrey died on 21 June 1949 at Kenneth Street, but that is far from being the end of the story.

At some point during these later years – and I am unable to say exactly when – all of Humphrey's photographic archive, assembled over more than half a century, was dumped in the Wick River and the sacks in which the material had been bagged carried into the harbour. This outrageous act of wanton vandalism resulted in a catastrophic loss of Caithness pictorial history, and the actions of whoever was responsible are utterly beyond belief and impossible to understand. There are those in Wick today who are in no doubt who committed what was a dreadful act, and one which has left the Wick Society in the interesting position of having copyright over Humphrey's pictures (given by his late daughter), while having virtually none of the actual photographs themselves. Thus, such of Humphrey's images which survive exist only between the pages of family photograph albums and in private collections.

S.S. "St. Clair," stranded at Wick
Photo by J. G. Humphrey   Published by J. George & Son, Wick

For various reasons the dating of some of these photographs has been difficult, and particular images may be earlier than indicated in the text. The postcard above was mailed in 1903, but the photograph featured is thought to date from January 1895. This was printed in reduced format to accommodate the message on the front, while the back was reserved wholly for the address.

I have always considered that the pre-eminence of the Johnston family photographers in Wick, together with the fact that to the best of my knowledge Humphrey's life has never been documented in any way, has resulted in his achievements being overshadowed, sidelined and neglected, their true worth unappreciated. My hope is that this introduction might help to rehabilitate the very considerable reputation of a photographer who is largely forgotten – but deserves to be better known – to the ranks of the greats in the Highlands and Islands where he properly belongs. For this reason, and because of local interest in certain quarters, I have selected Humphrey images wherever possible to illustrate the text (as these will be unknown to many) in the expectation that his pictures will be better appreciated and brought to the attention of a wider audience.

A Caithness guidebook issued between the wars extols the virtue of Wick's 'wonderfully pure air and its marked tonic qualities' and continues almost lyrically that 'the tingling ozone mingles with the sweet moorland air derived from the interior of Caithness, and the result is something which no one who takes a walk in the environs of Wick can fail to enjoy'. In fact, health grounds were the cause of bringing **John Cyril Percy Adams** to live in Wick after resigning his commission at the end of the Second World War. Born in London on 19 October 1911, Adams entered the world of photography through the RAF photographic school at Farnborough in the late 1920s. His subsequent work in air reconnaissance took him as far afield as the North-West Frontier of India, but more importantly and nearer home, he was engaged on secret missions of vital national importance in Europe during the Second World War.

In 1946 Adams acquired the former Humphrey studio at 4 River Street, and having completely modernised the premises reopened them as the Caithness Studio. Whereas his predecessor had relied on natural light for his portrait work, Adams introduced flash photography for all occasions, including weddings, which made him the fashionable photographer of his day. His friendship with David Oag, then editor of the *John O' Groat Journal*, saw his photographs frequently appearing in that newspaper, helping to keep Caithness in the forefront of the national news. Queen Elizabeth, the late Queen Mother, purchased Barrogill Castle (the Castle of Mey) in 1952, and for the next 50 years she would spend part of each year in Caithness; for John Adams his greatest honour was to be asked by the Queen Mother to take pictures there.

Despite never intending to stay in Wick for more than a year or two, Adams remained for twenty years before subsequently moving to Pitlochry. There he traded for a time as the Highland Studio before retiring in 1976 to Ramsey on the Isle of Man. In 1989, Clive Richards of North of Scotland Newspapers visited him in retirement there and was shocked to learn that, before leaving Pitlochry, his friend had destroyed virtually all the photographic material amassed during his years in Caithness. He had apparently simply become bored with his old negatives, and just wanted to be rid of them. However, he had retained a small box of photographs of the Queen Mother which Clive eventually located after an extended search in his loft. John Adams died about 1995, but at least something was salvaged from this photographic débâcle: a little box of photographs with a royal connection is now safely under lock and key at 42 Union Street.

Pictures by the late John Adams have been selected for three locations in this book. Regrettably, I have been unable to make contact with either his son or daughter as I would have wished. Their whereabouts are unknown to me but, should they see this book, they may take some pleasure in knowing that their father's name has not been forgotten in Caithness.

ACKNOWLEDGEMENTS

A book of this nature draws together information from a wide variety of sources, both oral and written, and I am grateful to local residents who so readily gave their time and knowledge, especially: Robert Howden and Joy Corley (the Portland Estate Office, Berriedale); George Bethune (Dunbeath Heritage Centre) and Alan McIvor of Thurso.

I wish to acknowledge the considerable contribution of those who so readily gave generous assistance in bringing together information which enabled the compilation of the photographic portraits on pages 3–7: North of Scotland Newspapers for permission to quote from the obituary of Alexander Johnston, originally carried by the *John O' Groat Journal* on 26 June 1896; the Wick Society for the photograph of Alexander Johnston, and permission to reproduce photographs from the Johnston Collection and images by John Gemmell Humphrey from my own collection that are within their copyright; Gail Inglis of the North Highland Archive; Iain Sutherland, ex-chairman of the Wick Society, who provided much of the information concerning Humphrey, and made available details of family history supplied to Wick Library by John Humphrey, grandson of the photographer; and finally to Clive Richards for permitting the introduction to his book *The Queen Mother and Family at Home in Caithness*, published by North of Scotland Newspapers, to form the basis of the profile of John Adams, and who kindly factually checked this piece prior to publication. Thank you all.

Special thanks to my wife, Angela, not only for producing the manuscript once again, but also for her forbearance during my often lengthy disappearances in the field while either seeking someone in particular, or attempting to verify an elusive fact – sometimes even with success.

Footnote: In order to give credit to the photographers described above, and to assist in the ready identification of their work throughout the book, I have adopted a code which appears, where applicable, at the end of relevant captions, except where the photographer's name forms part of the caption itself: Johnston Collection (JC); J. G. Humphrey (JGH); J. C. P. Adams (JA).

THE NORTH SEA COAST

Navidale Farm and Ord of Caithness.

Helmsdale, just inside the Sutherland border, is an appropriate place to commence the northward journey into Caithness. Historically, travel to this extreme north-eastern corner of mainland Britain had been accomplished only with difficulty in one of two ways: by sea (the more usual option), or on foot or pony over the Ord of Caithness, a 'green road' used for the movement of cattle and by pedlars and packmen. In medieval times pilgrims, too, passed this way to pay homage at the shrine of St Magnus in Kirkwall (Orkney). The route hugged the coast and had severe gradients which could prove formidable obstacles, especially in severe weather and in winter.

By 1811 that energetic engineer, Thomas Telford, was gradually edging his new road across the Ord and up the coast so that years later he was able to write: 'In the year 1828 a mail-coach passes daily from Tain by Bonar Bridge, the Fleet Mound, Dunrobin, Helmsdale and the Ord of Caithness to reach the extremity of the Island at Wick and Thurso without being interrupted by a single ferry'. Until 1972, when a new bypass and bridge was built over the River Helmsdale, the road to Wick had been by way of Telford's bridge of 1811 and Dunrobin Street, before joining the coast road. From Helmsdale the course of his road is both immediately and decidedly upward. Shortly the 'big house' of Navidale is glimpsed among trees on a cliff overlooking the North Sea. Navidale Farm (illustrated here) and the site of St Ninian's fifth century chapel are also seen on the seaward side; the bulky shape of the Ord of Caithness rises ahead.

The Ord poses no terrors for present-day travellers who may drive with ease over a route which has been immeasurably improved over the last 40 years. Although widened and re-engineered in places and known today as the A9, the general line of Telford's road remains. However, a century ago matters were very different. While the highest point marked on the Ordnance Survey map indicates a modest height of 747 feet, the sharp curves and steep gradients of the single-track road across the Ord presented very real challenges to the early motorists whose engines, brakes and tyres were put to severe tests. At a particularly dangerous point on the road a stone slab carried the grim inscription 'William Welch perished here, Be ye also ready', a chilling reminder to all who passed by, not only of the remoteness of the terrain, but also of the harsh weather conditions sometimes encountered on this headland.

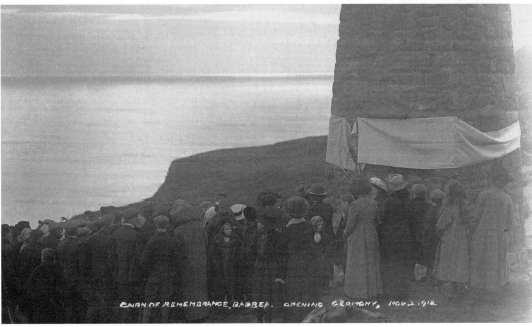

A little beyond the neatly grouped farm buildings at Ousdale (conspicuous by their isolation) lie the scant remains of Badbea, 'the village of birches'. The settlement was sited on sloping ground above precipitous cliffs, and came into being about 1804 when Sir John Sinclair of Ulbster cleared the surrounding area to make way for more profitable sheep. This was achieved by broad agreement with the local inhabitants, who expressed no interest in becoming shepherds, and in this respect was quite different from the forcible evictions which took place in neighbouring Sutherland. Life was hard for the dozen or so families (peak population totalled 100 in 1840) who built their simple stone and turf houses on the cliff using local grey and red granite. Each family possessed only the very barest essentials to sustain existence, and their unvarying diet consisted chiefly of potatoes and fish. Every house had a spinning wheel, whilst illicit stills were rife, as was smuggling. Cattle, chicken and children were tethered by the leg to rocks in order to prevent their falling over the nearby cliff while their parents worked the land or fished the plentiful haddock shoals off Badbea. Eventually the fishing failed and this small and once vibrant community died. Its ultimate fate was sealed when some families emigrated to the Antipodes to start a new life. *Top:* the abandoned village site showing the poignantly simple memorial constructed in 1911 from the stones of ruined houses. *Above:* Badbea briefly came alive with people again when Mrs George Gunn of Wick, whose forebears had resided here, unveiled the cairn on 2 November 1912. (JC)

Once across the Ord, the road to Berriedale and beyond lies through the Portland Estate. Travellers of old might reasonably have thought their troubles were behind them, but such notions would have been dispelled on reaching the top of Berriedale Brae, the first of two braes of the same name which have almost legendary notoriety. The steep and long descent is matched immediately by an equally severe uphill climb from Berriedale. Note the quite unique sign in the upper photograph (*c*.1920) which directs motorists in difficulty to cross the single lane road (with passing places) on to a rising track which would bring the vehicle to a halt – dangerous if traffic was approaching, but fortunately in those days cars were more of a rarity. To slow his descent to Berriedale, the 6th Duke of Portland was in the habit of attaching a piece of railway track (a sleeper, perhaps) to the rear of his motor car! *Above:* The Duke's Drive up to Langwell House diverges from the main road through woods (centre) said to be the finest in Caithness. (JGH)

Langwell House represents a mix of various building periods, with the oldest part dating from the eighteenth century. The turreted entrance, shown here prior to 1908, has long vanished. Sited on an elevated position, the house always came alive during August when the Duke and Duchess of Portland came north for the shooting season from their Welbeck Abbey Estate in Nottinghamshire. Prior to such visits, the gardeners would have carefully covered the best rose-heads for protection from inclement weather. Berriedale Brae was visible from the grounds, and when the Duke's car was spotted coming over the top, the protective coverings were quickly removed so that the blooms would present a perfect spectacle when the visitors arrived up at the house. Now those really were the days!

This group of buildings, photographed by John Humphrey in the 1920s, lies on what is now a bypassed loop of Thomas Telford's road; present-day traffic is carried over the new Berriedale bridges opened in 1963. The house (now the estate office for the 55,000 acre Langwell and Braemore Estates) was formerly an inn and mail coach change-house in the nineteenth century. The post office (left) is old-established and remains in use, while the other buildings have had various estate-related uses over the years e.g. stables, laundry etc. William Daniell, the famous artist and aquatinter whose pictures have an almost Grecian elegance, included an engraving of the inn and post office in his folio *A Voyage Round Great Britain*, c.1821.

Nearby, at a sharp bend on the old brae road (north) lies the former Berriedale smithy, which ceased working between the wars. In years past the gables have displayed a fine array of stags' heads, but more recently these have been missing from the left gable of the smithy. The sight of this photograph from the 1940s was of interest to the estate, and restoration of the missing antlers is expected soon, and may even have been undertaken by the time this book appears in print. Any sizeable estate required a large staff having a variety of skills, and some 47 people are recorded in employment a century ago when George King was factor. (JA)

Berriedale War Memorial.

'Their Name Liveth for Evermore'. Berriedale's war memorial is built of Kemnay (Aberdeenshire) granite and stands on a paved terrace between the old bridges where the Langwell and Berriedale Waters join on their run to the sea. The base is inscribed on three sides with the locations France–Belgium, Palestine–Salonika, and Egypt–Gallipoli. Commemorating the patriotism of the men of Berriedale and Braemore who gave their lives during the First World War, the memorial was unveiled by the Duchess of Portland on 25 September 1920 at a service of dedication attended by about 400 people.

Above: The crowd at the Langwell sheepdog trials, photographed by John Humphrey in the 1920s. This was an important annual event in the social calendar, and everyone is smartly turned out, with virtually every head covered. *Below:* Mill Road, Berriedale, showing Portland Terrace with well-stocked gardens and tidy frontages lining the riverbank. Estate workshops lie beyond the terrace, while the old meal mill, at the bend in the river, harnessed the conjoined Berriedale and Langwell Waters as they rushed to enter the sea (foreground). In 1858, Mr Huskinson's detailed survey undertaken for the 5th Duke of Portland described this little collection of buildings as 'a grinding mill, drying kiln, sawmill and wheelwright's shop, all recent erections worked by water power in good repair'. Milling has long ceased although the original machinery is still *in situ*. A swaying footbridge leads to the shore. (JGH)

'I suppose you will know that this is the Duchess's teahouse' is the message on this postcard sent from Berriedale Post Office on 31 January 1905. One can imagine Duchess Winifred spending many happy hours here as picnics were brought down the brae from the 'big house'. The little building stood just where the road ends in the previous photograph and looked across the bay. Estate papers record that the retaining wall was washed away by the sea in 1896, and subsequently the hut itself was carried away in a landslip. A little gem of a picture from days long gone.

The mid-nineteenth century would have seen thirteen boats fishing from this shore, and some of the women from Badbea (whose children were tethered for their own protection above the cliffs at home during their absence) found employment gutting fish here. On the small, flat promontory overlooking the sea, scant remains of a castle have been discovered, while the two Duke's Follies or 'Candlesticks' on the headland are said to have guided those at sea into the safety of the haven. The teahouse can be glimpsed (centre), along with the salmon bothy and former fisher cottages fronted by drying nets (right). These dwellings were vacated about 1950 and abandoned following incursions by the sea; now derelict and open to all weathers, they present a sorry spectacle. The ruins of an old ice house lie just out of sight. (JGH)

Right: Pointers at the Braemore Estate kennels photographed some time before the First World War. The highest peaks in the county are concentrated here, close to the Sutherland border: Maiden Pap (1,587 feet), centre; Morven (2,313 feet), right. Scaraben (2,055 feet) lies out of sight. Collectively these are referred to as the 'Heights of Caithness'.

Centre: Leaving Berriedale far below, a car carefully negotiates a sharp bend on the steep ascent over Berriedale Brae (north); beyond, towards Dunbeath, the motorist will encounter a plateau of undulating moorland. This area beyond the Ord forms part of the parish of Latheron which, at over 30 miles in length, has historically been known as 'The Long Parish' and is one of the largest in Scotland.

Below: J. B. White Ltd. of Dundee has encapsulated all the features so typical of this coast in this *c.*1935 photograph: a neatly cultivated landscape where sheep and cattle thrive. A century earlier the inhabitants of Badbea's cliff-top settlement would have come this way to sell their locally made items of birch wood, including baskets and corn flails, at the annual November market in Dunbeath.

Dunbeath Castle is perched on a rocky outcrop above the North Sea, and no one can say with certainty when the site was originally fortified, although the present building dates largely from the seventeenth century (with later additions and remodelling). Once a Sinclair stronghold, the castle featured fleetingly in the Civil War when the forces of Montrose, moving southwards from Orkney, obliged Lady Sinclair to surrender the castle after a brief siege in 1650. However, shortly thereafter the tables were turned on the 'Great Marquis' himself when he was defeated at the Battle of Carbisdale and imprisoned in the dungeon at Ardvreck prior to his execution in Edinburgh in May that same year. (JGH)

Dunbeath Village, the centre of a scattered community of croft and shore, *c*.1905. Among those who lived in this classically-built estate terrace were the estate factor, shopkeeper and miller, whose mill lay alongside the Dunbeath Water which flows close by. Traditionally, local crofts and the gardens (right) were dressed with a mixture of seaweed and fish-guts carted up from the shore – an excellent combination 'for giving ground heart'. The distinguished author Neil M. Gunn (1891–1973) was born two doors along the terrace from the hotel. His early education was received at the local school (now Dunbeath Heritage Centre), and the beauty of his childhood surroundings, the hills, and the working lives of crofters and fishermen are reflected in the intensity of his writing.

These pictures show Dunbeath Bay and Portormin Harbour in late Victorian times. The former importance of the herring fishing industry to the local economy can be gauged from the fact that seasonally some 3,000 additional migrant workers would be stationed here – fishermen, coopers, labourers, carters and the unsung heroines of the Scottish fishing industry, the lassies who gutted, graded and packed the 'silver darlings' into barrels (which were only ever used once). *Above:* The 'sea town' of Balcladich (sometimes Balacladich) sat uncomfortably close to the tideline – plainly too close – as during the mid-twentieth century incursions by the sea swept away this row of fishermen's dwellings. Portormin lies across the bay where the Dunbeath Water enters the sea. *Below:* Portormin Harbour was further developed in the last decade of Queen Victoria's reign, but there had been a harbour of sorts since at least 1800. By 1814 some 155 boats were based here. Various buildings, including the curing sheds, have vanished; those surviving include the early nineteenth century three-storied fishing store, the dome-roofed ice house and the salmon fishers' bothy where five men (who netted salmon from a coble at the river mouth) lived during the season.

'Your machine is now ready and I would be pleased to see you down any time that may be convenient.' On 1 August 1911, John Clark wrote this postcard to Mr Charles Sutherland of Achnaharish, Braemore. Clark, an engineer, established his motor and cycle repair business in this early prefabricated building by the roadside at Inver, just beyond Dunbeath. Local information suggests that this had originally been a show-stand purchased in Glasgow after one of the great exhibitions. Dr John Kennedy is standing to the left of the doorway, while aboard the Dunbeath, Latheron and Lybster coach are driver John MacAngus and his sister-in-law, Ina Bain. The building, somewhat modified and now derelict, has in more recent years served as a guest house.

About 150 years ago this building at Latheronwheel was very considerably expanded to become the 'big house' seen today. In 1835 Captain Robert Dunbar had laid out the small village along the road to the harbour, naming the new settlement 'Janetstown' after his mother, Lady Janet Duffus. This name appears widely on maps, including those of the Ordnance Survey, while Latheronwheel is also in common use

and is the name adopted in the *Caithness Official Guide* of years past. To complicate matters further, the building at the junction of the A9 and the harbour road – the Latheronwheel Hotel – displays a wall tablet denoting 'Janetstown 1853', thought to commemorate enlargement that year, so perhaps it should be renamed the Janetstown Hotel. I had hoped to resolve such anomalies and gauge local opinion, but the hotel was closed and for sale on my last visit, so this crisis of identity remains! (JGH)

Above: Built about 1726, the old packhorse bridge across the Latheronwheel Burn once provided an essential link for those travelling the route up and down the Caithness coast. Fishermen's stores and poles for drying nets are visible down by the harbour, and a ruined tower on the hill overlooks the scene. (JGH)

Below: Fortunately for us, John Humphrey photographed this building early last century when much more remained of the structure; only fragments survive today. The general belief is that this was a primitive lighthouse or landmark used as an aid for guiding returning boats safely into the harbour.

Latheronwheel Harbour is one of those finely constructed little havens which one comes to expect in a county having a long history and experience of working with local stone. In the mid-nineteenth century, at the height of the herring fishing boom, as many as 50 boats found refuge here. Near the angle of the far quay the door of a former ice house is visible, built into the hillside. The foreshore is now devoid of fishing paraphernalia and has been landscaped as a picnic area. Nowadays, only the ghosts of days past linger around this quiet corner of the Caithness coast. (JGH)

The opening ceremony for Latheron United Free Church, 1909; another fine study by John Humphrey. This is one of three local churches to be depicted here. Who could doubt that in former days Latheron was regarded as the ecclesiastical hub of 'The Long Parish'?

When in doubt, a call at the local post office can sometimes be fruitful. Latheron's sprightly elderly postmistress warmly welcomed me into her office – in reality no more than a room in a private house – the left one of the terrace (right), adjoining the junction with the Causewaymire Road to Thurso. A fire burned brightly in the grate as we discussed this view of the village taken a century ago. The former village school can be glimpsed (extreme right), but the large Free Church (centre), which at one time was supported by a considerable congregation, has long since been abandoned and is now extensively ruinous. On leaving, the postmistress told me proudly that she was a Gunn, a dominant clan hereabouts.

On a hill overlooking the North Sea stands the Old Parish Church of Latheron, which since 1985 has found a new use as the home of the Clan Gunn Heritage Centre and Museum. The church dates from the first quarter of the eighteenth century, and some of the Dunbeath Sinclairs are buried here. The centre also provides a base for the Clan Gunn Society worldwide, claiming 77 associated septs and maintaining links with clansmen through societies in North America, Nova Scotia and New Zealand. (JGH)

About 1800, following his return to the family estate after long service abroad with the Black Watch, Lt. General Sir Patrick Sinclair set about planning the new village of Lybster and developing the harbour. Main Street was built to join the coast road at right angles at an area named by the General as Quatre Bras (after Wellington's famous victory over Marshal Ney at the battle of 1815 in which his two sons had fought). *Top:* The Portland Arms, situated where these roads meet, has a long history of extending hospitality to travellers and grew in size when the stores (extreme right) were incorporated to enlarge the hotel. *Above:* The exceptional width of Main Street (seen *c.*1905) enabled the important annual Lybster three-day market to be held here, but this subsequently dwindled in size, and ultimately ceased, after being transferred to Black Park.

Right: Main Street *c.*1910, at the close of the elegant Edwardian era.

Centre: A contrived scene, most certainly, but Gunn's post office in Main Street (*c.*1906) would then, as now, have played a significant role in the lives of many, for in small communities this was not merely a business but also a meeting place where news and gossip would be exchanged.

Below: The Wick & Lybster Light Railway had a relatively short history, opening on 1 July 1903 and closing 41 years later despite a proposal during the Second World War to extend the line to Dunbeath. In April 1944 all stations and halts on the 13¾ mile route south of Wick were closed: Thrumster, Welsh's Crossing Halt, Ulbster, Mid-Clyth, Roster Road Halt, Occumster, Parkside Halt and Lybster. Lybster Station stood conveniently near the centre of the village, and the most commonly seen picture is that of the arrival of the inaugural train which prominently shows the engine and carriages, but obscures the station buildings themselves. As an alternative I have selected this early illustration showing a crowd of expectant passengers on the platform and the approaching train from Wick.

By way of the steep-sided bridge at Inver, the continuation of the road from Main Street winds down to Lybster Harbour, which has undergone a series of enlargements since General Sinclair first built a wooden pier at the mouth of the Reisgill Burn as part of his early plans for the settlement. These later harbour developments and the public buildings, large houses and farms which sprung up in the nineteenth century were financed from a flourishing economy based on wealth generated principally from the herring fishery. Traditionally, these migratory fish arrived off the coast between January and March and June to August. The boats would leave harbour in the early evening to drift with the shoals until about 4 a.m. when nets would be drawn. A swift return to port, followed by unloading and salting the catch, would see the itinerant fisher lassies gutting, grading and packing the fish into barrels. *Above:* Lybster Harbour from the north *c.*1895. By the mid-nineteenth century over 100 boats were based here, making Lybster one of the three most important herring stations in Scotland. *Below:* The harbour from the east *c.*1925. The group of former fishing stores (centre) have recently been restored and converted to house 'Waterlines', an informative visitor experience.

Shelligoe (Lybster) and Whaligoe (Ulbster) are prime examples of how every nook and cranny of the Caithness coast was adapted to exploit the herring fishery during the boom years 'when creels of silver herring [would] turn into creels of silver crowns'.

Access to the Whaligoe (whale 'geo' or inlet) Steps is alongside the early nineteenth century fishing station. Making the descent will not be appropriate for many, and great care must be exercised at all times. The Ulbster lands were once in the ownership of Sir John Sinclair, MP for Caithness, agricultural improver and patron of the local herring fishing industry. In 1790 Thomas Telford had declared Whaligoe 'a dreadful place', but that did not deter Sir John's tenant, Captain David Brodie, from blasting and clearing the little haven at a cost of £53. Further expenditure of £8 was incurred in cutting and constructing the stone stairway which zigzags up the previously unassailable cliff face. Estimates of the number of stone steps varies, and while I have seen numbers of between 338 and 365 mentioned, I have never felt able to count them individually myself, being more concerned with the preservation of life and limb! To stand in the harbour, from which sunlight is often largely excluded, where the cries of wheeling seabirds are magnified by the close, encircling cliffs and where the sea gently 'booms' in the surrounding caves and caverns, is an experience few could forget. In this natural and man-made wonder, one can only marvel that by 1850 there were 35 boats using this most improbable of harbours, and that the fisherwomen carried the catch in creels on their backs for sale in Wick, seven miles distant! (JA)

Three miles north of Whaligoe, Thrumster House stands at the end of a long wooded drive and, at the rear entrance, Wick photographer Alexander Johnston took this picture of a successful shooting party. The reverse of the photograph is printed 'A. Johnston, North of Scotland Photographic Rooms, Bridge Street, Wick'. This is of only limited help in attempting to apply an approximate date, but as Johnston moved into Brims' Buildings in Bridge Street about 1870, and the business transferred to Market Place about 1894, a reasonable assumption must be that the photograph was taken between these dates. Unfortunately I have been unable to establish the identities of any of those shown.

The village of Sarclet, seen here c.1905, was another development dating from about 1800 by Captain David Brodie – in this instance a linear crofting settlement above a sheltered sea inlet known as 'The Haven' – and another example of how every nook in the coastline was exploited to accommodate a few fishing boats. His wish to have the village known as 'Brodiestown' came to nothing.

Watten lies eight miles as the crow flies behind Wick, by a loch of the same name in the vast agricultural heartland of Caithness. This old-established meal mill, which once played such a vital role in local life and derived its water power from Loch Watten, dates from 1742. Rebuilding followed in 1840, and an extension was added in 1874. Although officially described only 70 years ago as 'a fine survival of another age', the old mill (now sadly without its mill-wheel and substantially ruinous) is currently used for hay storage.

Watten was the birthplace of Alexander Bain (1810–77) inventor of, *inter alia*, the electric clock. At the village crossroads (looking in the direction of Loch Watten *c*.1910) stands the tollhouse (right), built about 1815 on the Wick–Thurso road. The Brown Trout Hotel occupies the opposite corner today.

'How are you getting on with crochet?' asks Lizzie, the sender of this card posted at Watten Post Office on 4 November 1911. The addressee is a Miss Bain residing at Stirkoke House, 5½ miles down the road towards Wick. The house shown – described on this postcard as the Free Church Manse – still stands near the church among tall trees in the centre of Watten.

Regarded as a typical example of David Bryce's Scots baronial style, Stirkoke House was built for the Horne family in 1858/9. The most famous member of this family was General The Lord Horne of Stirkoke (1861–1929) who, during the First World War was recognised as the finest artillerist of his day – of any army – and who invented a military manoeuvre known as the 'creeping barrage'. He served with distinction on the Somme and Vimy Ridge, and led the British Army at the recapture of Mons. The General collapsed and died on 14 August 1929 while shooting over his Stirkoke Estate. After lying in state at Stirkoke Recreation Hall, the coffin was brought to the entrance of the big house (on the right in this picture) where, 'in the open, with the wind sighing in the trees and under a grey sky, a short but impressive funeral service was conducted'. Led by two horses and followed by a multitude of mourners on foot, the coffin was conveyed on a farm wagon from the house to Wick for burial. There, among scenes reported as being unprecedented, vast throngs paid tribute in eloquent silence as the cortège passed. A forlorn wood and encroaching vegetation along the former driveway now obscure the house, which has stood empty, neglected and abandoned for almost 40 years. Following a fire ten years ago the building only survives as a shell. The great days of Stirkoke have gone.

Left: Typical reactions of travellers on discovering the tinkers' caves near Wick *c.*1906 were: 'This is one of the caves we explored yesterday morning. We were quite surprised at seeing such a race of people living in our own civilised time', and, 'This is a tremendous cave on the shore near Wick where the tinkers, a lot of gipsy folk, find cover and shelter. They go about from place to place all over the country and get their food by begging at different farms. They are the most wild-looking creatures.'

Right: George Wallace Levack (1848–1922) was a blacksmith and self-styled 'Bard of the North' (a title disputed by his contemporaries). After leaving school at age thirteen, and having taught himself in the style of the great poets, Levack had three small volumes published. *What I saw inside the Fairies Hill* was his most famous poem, and describes his claimed attempted abduction by the fairies who lived at Fairy Hillock up the Wick River.

Those travelling the Caithness coast road northwards will notice increasingly that the scattering of Norse place-names intensifies, and from Wick onwards becomes a torrent in a land that is almost totally Norse in character and tradition. **Wick**, a royal, municipal and parliamentary burgh is the county town of Caithness, and in 1901 its population stood at 8,463. These are a few significant dates: *Eighth to thirteenth centuries:* settled by the Vikings, whose name for Wick was *Vik* (bay); earliest settlement north of the Wick River. *1140:* town referred to in the Sagas. *1588:* Wick sacked by the Earl of Sutherland. *1589:* King James VI grants charter and royal burgh status. *Early nineteenth century:* harbours developed at the mouth of the Wick River and at Pulteneytown (the latter built by the British Fisheries Society to Thomas Telford's plan) to exploit the herring and curing industries. *1860s:* the herring boom years with the golden promise of an endless Eldorado – Wick, 'Herringopolis', the largest herring port in the world. *1863/83:* huge sums spent in harbour expansion and improvements, and to rectify recurring storm damage. *1874:* Wick linked with Inverness by Highland Railway. *1917:* the enormous wealth generated by exports of salted herring ended almost overnight due to the First World War and the Russian Revolution which resulted in vast debts and widespread bankruptcies.

Francis Street looking north from the entrance to West Park. This colour-tinted postcard, featuring a Johnston photograph, was mailed from Wick Post Office on 1 August 1904 and is unique among my Johnston images in bearing on the reverse the imprint of a small rubber stamp reading 'Printed in Austria'. The large West Church has since been demolished, and the site is currently occupied by petrol pumps and a car showroom.

Dempster Street at the junction with Francis Street, 1909. The flooding was very probably caused by excessive storm water-levels carried by the Luteskerry Burn which runs underground at this point. (JGH)

Breadalbane Terrace in Pulteneytown, seen from Pulteney Post Office, *c*.1905. The name of Sir William Pulteney, Thomas Telford's patron and a Governor of the British Fisheries Society, is perpetuated in this residential and harbour development undertaken a century earlier, and built largely with local stone quarried at South Head. Lower Pulteneytown and the harbour are reached by a wide flight of steep steps known as the Blackstairs.

Wick Harbour *c*.1906. 'An afternoon walk along the coast to the "Trams" [The Brig o' Trams – a natural rock bridge from the mainland to a pillar in the sea] when the legion of fishing boats with their dark-red bellying sails is radiating from the narrow harbour, is a unique experience which everyone with a soul for animated picturesqueness will enjoy.' (M. J. B. Baddeley's *Thorough Guide*, 1885.)

In 1862, 1,122 boats were based in the harbour giving employment to 3,800 fishermen during the herring fishing season (which lasted from about the third week in June until the first week of September); a further 4,000 ancillary workers were based ashore. At such times Wick's resident population could more than double in size. Three years later, Alexander Johnston set up his heavy, cumbersome camera equipment to take two plates making a complete panorama of the harbour; this is one of them. Placed side by side, the two produce a truly amazing scene – one of the classic masterpieces of the Scottish fishing industry – which may be seen in the Wick Society's Heritage Centre in Bank Row. Herringopolis indeed!

Sail and steam jostle for position to take the tide c.1905. From 1874, the fishermen of Wick were among the first in Scotland to use large steam trawlers. (JC)

Wick Bay panorama from Scalesburn as boats wait for the tide to enter Pulteneytown Harbour. (JC)

Another classic photograph taken just prior to the First World War, showing a number of fishing port abbreviations on the sides of the vessels including: A (Aberdeen); BF (Banff); BCK (Buckie); and WK (Wick). Activity on a scale such as this will never be seen again. Walking around these eerily silent quays today one can so easily imagine the sounds of the past: from the curing and coopering sheds, of catches being unloaded, the fisher lassies gutting at their farlins, the clatter of horses' hooves and the rumble of the wheels of herring-laden carts. These sights and sounds may have gone, but the ghosts of the past are palpable. (JC)

Top: What a haul – a multitude of the 'silver darlings' in the hold and right across the deck – with hardly room for one more! (JGH) *Above:* The herring leave the hold in baskets, each having a capacity of approximately 7 stone (98 lbs). Four baskets equalled a cran, the traditional measure for herring. When the fishing was good such scenes gave some credence to the claim that – during the season – no less than 500 gallons of whisky were consumed *each day* in Wick. (JGH)

Landing the catch opposite Rose Street. 'It's a sight to see the fishing boats come in here. Men and women all work the same and they say earn jolly good money', wrote a visitor to Wick on 14 July 1914. The First World War, destined to change everything, was only days away, and nothing would ever be the same again. (JGH)

In the 1860s there were 94 fish-curing firms in Wick. The letters JMP stamped on the barrels at this Shaltigoe curing yard stood for James More of Pulteneytown. Around Wick Bay some of the more prominent curers were Joe Calder; Davidson's of Leith; Water's; Sinclair & Buchan; Jock MacLeod; and the Anglo Russian Curing Company. The Scottish export trade of salted herring to Ireland and the slave plantations in the West Indies was immense, while after the Napoleonic Wars (post 1815) the European market flourished with huge exports to the Baltic states, Eastern Europe, the German states and Russia. Total production rose from 90,000 barrels in 1811 to one million in 1873, increasing further throughout the late nineteenth century. (JC)

'The scene by the harbour-side where the herring are landed in baskets, disembowelled and packed in barrels by strangely-attired women, called 'gutters', at a rate of nearly 30 a minute, is for the curious rather than the sensitive.' (M. J. B. Baddeley, 1885.)

While some fisherwomen worked at only one port for the season, others following the herring shoals on their annual clockwise migration around the British Isles might find themselves working in a variety of locations between Ireland, the Isle of Man, the Outer Hebrides and the West Coast, Shetland, the Moray ports, Aberdeen and down to Great Yarmouth and Lowestoft. At the start of the season many travelled more than 100 miles overland from the West Coast to Wick, taking a week to make the journey *on foot*. They lived and slept in insanitary bothies, sometimes a dozen or more to a room. The stench in the streets around the harbour of 'putrescent effluvia from fish offal' was overpowering. Long hours (usually working in teams of three – two gutting and one packing), spent in the open without any protection from the elements, was their lot. Often ankle-deep in fish-guts, they were themselves so spattered with blood, grease and fish-scales as to be almost unrecognisable. Their fingers were bandaged for protection against cuts and the effects of the coarse salt with which they worked. Experienced girls could gut 30–60 fish a minute as they deftly wielded their sharp knives. The photograph shows a deep farlin (gutting trough) which made back-breaking work for the gutters; later, sloping farlins were introduced. Earnings were liable to fluctuation and dependent on various factors including numbers of barrels packed, volumes of fish landed and the state of the export markets. In the late nineteenth century a really good season might yield as much as £15 for the fisher girls.

A barrel took 850–1,000 herring packed layer upon layer in salt; the process of sinkage (shrinkage) was rectified over 21 days by two 'fillings-up', following which a cooper secured the lid. Before export, a fisheries officer inspected the barrels to ensure the curer's name was visible, picked random samples to verify the size and quality stated, and if satisfactory the barrel received the Crown Brand mark (with the word FULL below), a universally recognised guarantee that indicated the herring were up to standard for both quality and quantity. Foreign buyers also inspected before purchasing, removing lids at random and sometimes even taking a bite from the back of a raw herring! Selling abroad was effected either through a commission agent at an agreed price, or by direct shipment. The former method was favoured by many as the price was firm, whilst direct shipment could prove volatile with variable funds resulting at times of shortage or glut.

Right: Packing herring, Wick.

Centre: Taken on a summer's afternoon in 1929, this photograph shows the yards left shipshape and devoid of activity, probably at a weekend. The pilots' house (extreme left) overlooks the harbour.

Below: The Stevenson family were evidently not enamoured with Wick. Robert Louis Stevenson (of *Treasure Island* fame) stayed in Harbour Terrace, Pulteneytown, in the autumn of 1868. This experience prompted him to write some less than flattering comments about the town, but despite these the Literary Society of Wick placed a plaque on the house in 1907. A stone's throw away, his father, Thomas Stevenson, engineer to the Northern Lighthouse Board, had commenced the building of this breakwater during 1863 in what became a life and death struggle with the elements. After continuous attacks by the sea and the expenditure of £100,000 over a ten year period, the project was abandoned following the severe storms of 1872; only an iron pole protruding above the water marks the spot today. This humiliating reverse is said to have haunted the renowned engineer and builder of lighthouses for the rest of his life. (JC)

THE HARBOUR, WICK

BUILDING THE BREAKWATER

Throughout history, the relationship between Man and the sea has, at best, been an uneasy truce. The seas surrounding the rugged coast of this most north-easterly corner of mainland Britain have not only yielded up great wealth, but also at times exacted a terrible cost in the loss of lives and shipping. Recurring poundings by wind and waves often resulted in damage to the Wick quays and piers which have absorbed a mint of money since being built – so perhaps Thomas Stevenson should not have been too hard on himself. High tides accompanied by strong easterlies can be a fatal combination, as shown by these scenes prior to the First World War. (JGH and JC)

Storms and floods occurred with depressing frequency. *Top:* In November 1909 the Wick River was in a
fearsome state. John Humphrey's photographic studio in River Street was located conveniently close by, and
he would have been immediately on hand to take this photograph. *Above:* Watched by a small crowd, residents
of Alexandra Place (Whitechapel) salvage belongings on 13 June 1931.

The following few examples are representative of the many photographs of large processions and crowds marking royal occasions, the annual Lifeboat Day (held in the first week of January) and Herring Queen parades. Most sections of such processions, including the decorative floats, were captured on film by Messrs Johnston and Humphrey, and the images largely speak for themselves. Such events were great expressions of civic pride.

Lifeboat Day 1910 and 1912. The lower picture shows a float in Argyle Square. (JC)

The election of the Herring Queen and her attendants was a celebration of the herring on which the prosperity of Wick had once depended. As might be expected, the Queen arrived by boat in the harbour and, after an official welcome, toured the town. *Top:* The Queen of 1938 was Alice Taylor (then aged 15), whose blue dress was decorated most appropriately with sequins representing fish-scales. Her attendants seen aboard the float in Northcote Street were (left to right): Annie Durrand, Margaret Bain, Crista Taylor and Isobel Cormack. *Below:* The 1938 parade enters Bridge Street. By 1953 the herring had vanished and, as a natural consequence, the celebration was discontinued. (Unattributed but both believed JC.)

As Queen Victoria's record-breaking reign came to an end and a new century dawned, a reversal in the economic fortunes of Caithness took place. The fishing became variable, there was much unemployment, and the final hammer-blow came when a number of local quarries closed. These circumstances combined to produce another wave of emigration (nothing new in the history of the Highlands and Islands) as there was no alternative employment. In this 1912 photograph crowds gather on the platforms as the 8.40 a.m. train for Inverness waits to leave Wick with emigrants bound for Canada. Once there the new arrivals would write home to provide an address for friends and relatives. This often prompted the sending of a postcard showing scenes of the departure from Wick Station, and bearing messages such as this humorous one, written from 26A Vansittart Street: 'I suppose Toronto is a right swanky place; it will be almost like Wick, and nearly as big'. (JGH)

Another poignant scene as soldiers march through the town on 6 August 1914 on their way to war with Germany. At this time many were convinced that all would be over in a matter of weeks, but such talk faded quickly as the largest armies the world had ever seen (before or since) pounded each other across the muddy, waterlogged and shell-torn landscapes of Northern France and Flanders in total stalemate. The resultant huge loss of life and limb was on a scale never previously experienced in military conflict. (JC)

The windows of Rosebank House looked down on the scene on 31 October 1923 when General The Lord Horne of Stirkoke, the local war hero to whom General Haig had paid tribute, presided over the unveiling of the memorial to those who fell in the conflict of 1914–18. Miss Adelaine Florence Henderson died on 24 October 1927 leaving Rosebank House (her family home) and its grounds, together with a legacy, to the Wick and Pulteneytown District Nursing Association for the purpose of establishing, equipping and partially endowing a nursing home in Wick to be known as 'The Henderson Memorial Nursing Home' in memory of her sisters and herself. The site was later developed as the Caithness General Hospital. (JC)

The 50 bedroom Station Hotel dates from 1866 and was well-established by the time the railway opened in 1874. Conveniently located near the station, the new hotel would have provided some competition to the older, but smaller, Caledonian Hotel further along the opposite (east) side of Bridge Street. Mr Randall, whose name appears prominently on the building itself, became the proprietor of the Station Hotel in 1896. This view dates from 1905, prior to the erection of a large and distinctive iron and glass entrance porch (illustrated in the pictures on the facing page). This was removed when the Station Hotel found a new use as a nursing home some years ago.

Above: A superb advertising postcard issued by the Station Hotel during the proprietorship of W. Hatje in the 1920s. Domestic staff peer out on to Bridge Street from a first floor window. Beyond, over the Wick River, is Rosebank House. (JGH)

Centre: Bridge Street, 1914. The wide bridge in the foreground was built in 1877 to replace an earlier one. Some fine, classical public buildings are seen, right: the Commercial Bank (built 1830) and beyond, the town hall (1828, topped by a clock and elongated cupola). The Sheriff Court of 1866 is out of view.

Right: The business of David Cormack (watchmaker, jeweller and optician) at 11 Bridge Street was established in 1850 and is seen here *c.*1904. Although the family connection ceased about fourteen years ago, his name is still shown above the door.

High Street bedecked with flags on Coronation Day, 1902. King Edward VII succeeded to the throne on the death of Queen Victoria in January 1901. His coronation had been carefully planned and arranged for June the following year, but serious illness caused a postponement until 9 August. To commemorate the event, his first act was to present Osborne House in the Isle of Wight to the nation (a house much loved by his mother, but one which he hated).

Plenty of activity in High Street as several buses load with goods and passengers, a scene which serves to emphasise the importance of Wick as the hub of vital transport links with outlying Caithness. A bus for Thurso (right) is loading outside the *Northern Ensign* office (bookseller, stationer, printer and bookbinder), and older residents will note other well-known businesses including Fred Shearer who advertised 'smart wear for smart women', and Greenlees 'Easiephit' shoe shop (centre), next door to which in Market Place was Johnston's photographic studio (out of sight). In 1929 (the date of this picture) a bottle of Johnnie Walker Red Label Scotch Whisky cost 12/6d and a jar of Robertson's Silver Shred Marmalade 7½d, while in Shearer's, a Viyella nightie might be priced 17/11d.

Opened in 1926, the New Pavilion Cinema had originally been a roller-skating rink (*top*, JGH), and in an advertisement that year the facilities were described as 'the most commodious and luxurious place of entertainment in the North of Scotland'. There were over 650 upholstered tip-up seats in the hall and gallery, a modern gas-heating system had been specially installed by the Wembley Heating Co. of London, and two of the latest type of cinematograph machines were used for projection of films. Piano and violin music was played at all performances. Bookings for 1927 included all the best and latest pictures with films changed three times weekly. Admission prices (including tax) were 5d, 9d, and 1/3d. The premises, a nightclub in later years, were gutted by fire in 1996.

North Public School, Wick, at the top of Shore Lane about 1907. While some external features have changed, the building is still recognisable today. However, the pupils have long gone to be replaced by British Telecom stores and a workshop, while the playground which once rang with shouts and laughter is now silent, having become a car park for the company's fleet of vehicles.

North Shore, Wick, *c.*1905.

In 1909 John Humphrey attended the unveiling of this monument conspicuously sited on the north shore of Wick Bay. The inscription reads 'To perpetuate the patriotism of those natives of Caithness who served their country on land and sea. Many of their names, rescued from forgetfulness, are preserved for posterity in this memorial tower. Their names are here: their deeds are in the histories of the world.' Various campaigns are detailed around the tower's base.

Two miles north-east of Wick a minor road ends among some eighteenth century fishermen's stores set above a sheltered, narrow haven having a shelving beach, quay and small jetty. Perhaps the road originally started from here, for this is Staxigoe, said to be the birthplace of the Caithness herring fishing industry and a place whose importance in times past could be gauged by the fact that mail for Wick had to be addressed 'by Staxigoe'. About 1767 three local fishermen began fishing for herring in a small way, but 23 years later 200 boats landed fish at Staxigoe, Broad Haven and Wick over a period of sixteen weeks. The good times came to an end in 1924 when the export of cured herring ceased here. *Below:* Stranded whale (length 60 feet, weight 50 tons) at Staxigoe, 1923. (Both photographs unattributed, but believed JC.)

Until 1933 travel to Caithness had been undertaken by one of three methods: by sea; overland by the coastal route; or by rail, but that year a fourth alternative was added when a small airport was opened at Hillhead, Wick. The *Caithness Official Guide* of the period announced that 'for speed and novelty, advantage may be taken of the air service which conveys its passengers direct from Inverness to Wick'. *Above:* A Highland Airways plane at Wick with mail and passengers from Inverness, *c.*1934. (JC) *Below:* Leaving for Inverness ('the Highland Capital'). (JC)

A minor road ends abruptly at Ackergillshore on Sinclair's Bay. Quite extraordinarily, and despite having had no lifeboat based here since the early 1930s, this tiny settlement can claim two related distinctions: the earliest surviving lifeboat house in the Highlands (built 1878), and a ferro-concrete slipway claimed to be the first of its type in Britain, constructed in 1910. Here, crowds throng the shore at the opening ceremony of the new slipway that year. (JC)

Many ships have gone to their graves around this north-east corner of mainland Britain, where the long coastlines of Caithness protrude into the huge expanse of the North Sea, an area fabled for wild seas, strong currents, sudden squalls, and for dangerous reefs and skerries. The SS *Indian* of Liverpool (a Leyland Line ship) came to grief near Gibbs Craig at Duncansby Head in thick fog and, shadowed by the Huna lifeboat (just visible amidships), made Sinclair's Bay where she settled bow first. Her cargo was rock salt, a valuable commodity used variously as table salt, in a number of manufacturing processes and as a fertilizer. (JGH)

Ackergill Tower sits almost on the shore of the wide sweep of Sinclair's Bay and is believed to date from the fifteenth century (but was substantially rebuilt in 1851); records indicate that an even earlier fortification stood here. In 1698 Ackergill passed to the Dunbars of Hempriggs (later the Duff-Dunbars of Hempriggs and Ackergill), an important local family owning adjoining estates which included the lands of Wick. In 1803 Sir Benjamin Dunbar provided 390 acres of land to enable Thomas Telford to plan the new fishing settlement at Pulteneytown. In August 1916 Lt. Cdr. Kenneth Duff-Dunbar, an early submariner, lost his life when his submarine was reported missing; the vessel's whereabouts remained a mystery until located near Heligoland in 2001. Duff-Dunbar never saw his son and heir (also Kenneth) who was born three weeks after his father's death. In an echo of his father's fate, Kenneth lost his life in Normandy nine days after D-Day in 1944 and, with his passing, the Dunbar title came to an end. Today, Ackergill operates as a business and hospitality centre, and although the old family ties are broken I believe a room there has been devoted to Duff-Dunbar and naval memorabilia.

The Keiss Hotel, shown here c.1930 in landlord James Miller's time, has since been renamed the Sinclair Bay Hotel.

Top: The neatly developed grid pattern layout of Keiss, which lies between the Wick to John O' Groats road and the harbour, is well illustrated by this aerial photograph. The harbour, built about 1830 by local engineer and shipbuilder James Bremner, also features a fishermen's store on the quay and an ice house (extreme right). In 1855, 50 vessels were based here crewed by a total of 180 men. (Photograph reproduced here by kind permission of Aerofilms.com.) *Above:* One can only but admire the masonry, for like so many others throughout the county this is an exquisitely built small harbour, designed and constructed by Caithness men who had a long history of working with local stone. Herring have given way to large quantities of partans often landed here, with the result that the village was referred to as the 'crab capital' of the county between the wars.

The old and the not quite so old stand within a stone's throw of each other. Built on the north side of Sinclair's Bay about 1600, Old Keiss Castle (seen here *c.*1891) is one of a number of fortifications ringing this coast, and appears at first glance to be an integral part of the cliff itself. The most significant event in the castle's history took place in 1679 when George Sinclair attempted to legitimise his claim to the Earldom of Caithness by forcibly occupying the very seat of power at Girnigoe Castle, near Noss Head. His actions proved a disaster for not only was he expelled from Girnigoe, but also from his own seat at Keiss. From that year onwards the castle has gently decayed, hastened by the occasional crumbling of the cliff. Keiss House, which has stood within sight of the castle since 1755, underwent a complete transformation in the extravagant Scots baronial style of David Bryce in the 1860s, since when it has generally been referred to as Keiss Castle.

Norway is only 300 miles from the northern tip of mainland Britain, and the Vikings once occupied Orkney and Shetland in addition to this part of Scotland. At Freshwick, four miles from Duncansby Head, Norse influence remains almost tangible. Buchollie Castle has the reputation of being the keep of Sweyn, a notorious twelfth century Norse pirate whose adventurous life is chronicled in the *Orkneyinga Saga*.

Buchollie Castle

Wife Geo (spelt 'Goe' on this postcard caption) is said to be the best example of its kind in Britain.

WIFE GOE, near DUNCANSBY HEAD, CAITHNESS.

This coastal structure has been cut out by the sea from bedded flagstone cliffs of Old Red Sandstone age. It illustrates the formation of goes or cañon-like fissures, and of sea-caves, by the erosive action of the waves along vertical planes of weakness in the rocks.

Geological Survey and Museum, London. No. B.872

Many superb examples of natural erosion and weathering can be viewed around the Caithness coast: geos, arches, caves, pillars and rock bridges. These extraordinary witch's hat-like formations, the famous Duncansby Stacks, have been formed over infinite time by the unceasing action of the sea. (JGH)

DUNCANSBAY STACKS

Duncansby Head is to Caithness what Cape Wrath is to Sutherland: a turning point for mariners. However, unlike the latter, whose lighthouse was operational by 1828, Duncansby had to wait until 1924 for its headland to be lit. Somewhat unusually, the tower is square rather than round, and John Humphrey was here with his camera to photograph the construction phase. The light has a range of 22 miles and looks across the Pentland Firth, the 'Northern Gate' between Scotland and Orkney where Atlantic Ocean and North Sea meet. The ebb and flow of these waters creates fast-moving currents (flowing at 10–12 mph), eddies, overfalls and fierce tidal races, each having an exotic name: the Bore of Huna, the Wells of Tuftalie, Duncansby Bore, the Rispie and the Merry Men of Mey – and if they were not enough there is a fearsome whirlpool off Stroma's north end. Little wonder that in the days of sail the Firth was known as 'hell's mouth'.

These waters have been known to seafarers for millennia: the Vikings, the Romans, and Phoenician traders who came this way 1,000 years before Christ. Pytheas, the Massilian Greek explorer and navigator, rounded the headland in the fourth century BC on his way to 'discovering' Iceland. Significantly, his bireme was piloted by men from Caithness who already knew the way.

THE PENTLAND COAST

Situated a mile or so to the west of Duncansby Head, John O' Groats is today an internationally famous location and the goal of so many tourists who have made this spot the most photographed place in Caithness. Why should this be, for John O' Groats is neither the most north-easterly nor northerly point of mainland Britain? The simple fact is rather mundane: the road north of Latheron and Wick (formerly the A9 and renumbered the A99 in recent years), ends here overlooking the Pentland Firth and Orkney. The distance between John O' Groats and Land's End in Cornwall is, at approximately 880 miles, the greatest distance between any two points linked by road on the British mainland, and this has attracted various 'end to end' record-breaking attempts by conventional and sometimes distinctly unconventional forms of travel: among these motoring, cycling, walking, relay-running and even pram-pushing. All have their records! Such events have been newsworthy down the years, and in the public imagination John O' Groats and Land's End are firmly coupled together with, of course, the John O' Groats House Hotel featuring either at the start or the conclusion of each epic feat of endurance and stamina. From the extensive selection of pictorial material available, I have chosen this isolated and windswept image of 1891 showing the hotel as originally built and which had been opened by the Prince of Wales, later Edward VII, seventeen years earlier. At that time the settlement had no jetty, and 45-foot herring boats operated from the shore. Needless to say, the years since 1891 have witnessed much change brought about by the commercial pressures of our age. This small community by the edge of the sea plays host to botanists, ornithologists, admirers of fine coastal scenery and, of course, increasing numbers of curious visitors whose northern itinerary inevitably includes this tourist destination.

But what of the name John O' Groats? Three Dutch brothers, of which the senior was apparently Jan (John) de Groot (or Grot, spellings vary), settled here in the late fifteenth century, farming the land and operating the ferry to Orkney, the payment for the passage then being a groat, some say. Over time the de Groots multiplied, with eight branches of the family having that name. Inevitably disputes arose over the family hierarchy, and who was entitled to sit at the head of the table at the annual celebration of their original arrival in Scotland. John eventually provided a clever solution by building an eight-sided house having eight separate entrances which gave access to an octagonal table: therefore, all were treated equally and none could claim to be above the other. Tradition relates that the mound and flagstaff near the hotel mark the site of the Dutchman's famous house.

To conclude this introduction to John O' Groats, a short passage written by that indefatigable traveller and author, H. V. Morton, comes to mind. After a wearying day's travel he had reached Wick 'as twilight was beginning to darken into night', and he still had to complete the final leg of his journey to the John O' Groats House Hotel, seventeen miles distant. Eventually, in total darkness, he approached his destination noting that the lighthouse at Duncansby Head was 'sweeping a yellow sword over the Pentland Firth, and there were other lights too, as the jagged headlands of Scotland gave their warning to the night'. Despite the late hour of his arrival, he received a warm welcome and an offer of food. 'And, when I had eaten, I went up to a small room where a fire of peats was burning in the grate, filling the room with the smell of Gaeldom, reminding one of Connemara and Arisaig.' (*In Scotland Again*, H. V. Morton, 1933.) Hospitality indeed!

Such a picture, showing the famous seat, was always one for the family photograph album, providing proof to relatives and friends that one had really visited the renowned John O' Groats.

The hotel's octagonal tower perpetuates the shape of John de Groot's much earlier house, and further emphasis is given to this theme by an eight-sided table, the centrepiece of the elegantly furnished Edwardian smoking room.

SMOKING ROOM
JOHN O'GROATS HOTEL

"John O'Groats House Hotel."   Published by J. George & Son Wick.

Hubert Wingfield Egerton, seen here with his American-built Locomobile steam car in 1900, was an early motoring pioneer, although not the first to accomplish an 'end to end' run. That distinction fell to Henry Sturmey, the first editor of the *Autocar*, driving a twin cylinder Daimler three years earlier. Egerton's car consumed 26 gallons of water every 20 miles but because so many functions required constant attention, he failed even to cross the boundary into Sutherland on his first day at the wheel! (JC)

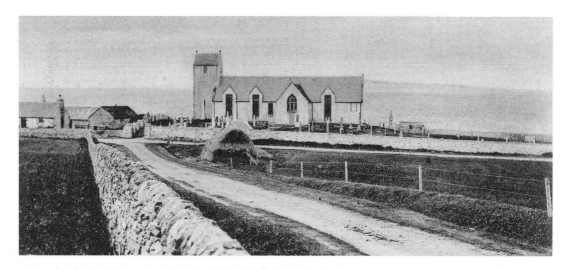

Canisbay consists of a cluster of houses surrounded by a crofting and farming township at the hub of a group of smaller districts – Seater, Gills, Warse and Brabster. The dignified Old Church of Canisbay is a pre-Reformation building standing on the site of an earlier church built in the twelfth century; there are many noteworthy memorials in the churchyard. Like several other churches along this coast, the distinctive square tower above Gills Bay has acted down the centuries as a landmark to mariners navigating their course around the dangerous waters of the Pentland Firth. John Adams took the interior photograph above *c.*1950.

Since John de Groot was laid to rest in Canisbay, his tombstone has undergone substantial restoration, has seen several changes of location, and may currently be found in the church vestibule. The quaintly lettered inscription, written in the first person, states that John's son Donald 'laid me here April 13 Day, 1568'. There is no doubt that the family was important locally, particularly as successive members worked the Orkney ferry for nigh on 250 years.

This substantial two-storied nineteenth century building has an enviable situation looking down to the Old Church of Canisbay and across the sea to the island of Stroma. The doorway a little beyond the rather ornate cast iron porch is the entrance to the post office, while the village hall lies in the background behind the car. Today, Canisbay Post Office continues to serve the local community, and the scene has changed little since this picture was taken some 70 years ago.

The turbulent waters of the 'Stormy Pentland' have no regard for shipping and claimed another victim in October 1910 when the SS *Malin Head* ran aground at the Ness of Quoys (Canisbay). Owned by the Ulster Steamship Company of Belfast, she was bound for Montreal with a cargo of pig-iron which had been loaded at Middlesborough. Although she subsequently became a total loss, much of the cargo was salvaged. (JGH)

CASTLE OF MEY NEAR JOHN O'GROATS

PHOTO –
SCOTTISH SUNDAY
EXPRESS
B 9801

The Castle of Mey is an ancient seat of the Earls of Caithness situated three miles west of Canisbay. Having acquired the Barony of Mey from the Bishop of Caithness in 1566, George, the 4th Earl, commenced the original building of substance here – a defensive four-storied tower which was not completed until 1589. In 1572 George granted a charter of the Mey lands to his second son William, who became the 1st Laird of Mey. Although the Sinclairs of Mey had a colourful (and sometimes violent) past, their stewardship of this northern estate continued until 1889 when the 15th Earl of Caithness died without issue.

In August 1952, following the death of her husband, King George VI, the late Queen Mother acquired the small and compact castle, then known as Barrogill Castle, for a reputed sum of £26,000. At that time the building was in an advanced state of dilapidation which, but for her intervention, could have proved terminal. Lighting was provided only by candles and oil lamps, and the sole source of heating came from open peat fires. Such facilities as bathrooms were totally absent and had yet to be introduced to this sixteenth century building. Externally, the unkempt gardens verged on the wild. Over time all the amenities were brought into the twentieth century, and the castle's 30 rooms furnished with works of art, antiques (some of which were obtained locally) and family items reflecting the owner's royal status – all of which created an atmosphere of elegance and informality.

The care and attention lavished on the fabric of the castle (the name of which reverted to the Castle of Mey) was extended to the 50 acres of policies and gardens, sections of which were filled with flowers and vegetables raised behind high walls and hedges for protection from the often severe winds experienced along the exposed Pentland Coast. The breeding of prize-winning herds of sheep and Aberdeen Angus cattle became one of the Queen Mother's many interests, an activity which still continues. In short, the Castle of Mey became her Caithness retreat – the only home she ever owned privately – and until her death in 2002 part of each year was spent here. In 1996 she handed over the property to a charitable trust, with the result that the castle and grounds are now open to the general public during the summer months. Overlooking the magnificent Caithness coast and the ever-changing panorama of the Pentland Firth and Orkney, this former royal residence (pictured here c.1953) is certain to find a place on every tourist's itinerary. (Photograph reproduced here by kind permission of Express Newspapers.)

Above: Barrogill Lodge, Mey, *c.*1930.

Centre: Berriedale Arms Inn and, beyond, Mey Post Office. The inn has long provided hospitality to those travelling the north coast road between Thurso and John O' Groats, and in recent years has undergone a change of name to the Castle Arms Hotel, brought about, according to the proprietor, by tourists planning their journeys from afar confusing the location with Berriedale on the Ord of Caithness. The curved ironwork over the porch surmounted by a crowing cock which formerly carried the old name has been altered to reflect the change. Mey Post Office has vanished from the scene, having been incorporated into the hotel.

Left: The indifferent state of the road at Mey, looking east, with the inn and post office identified by a cross. Both postcards date from *c.*1905 and were mailed through the post office shown.

From Mey a loop from the main road leads to Harrow Harbour (once a place of great activity in the flagstone industry) and Scarfskerry, which an old *Caithness Guide* informs us 'has an intimate association with the sea, having bred a number of sea-captains'. In these lands heavy with grain, the local miller was a key individual, and his universal disappearance has left many a former mill derelict in the countryside. The Mill of Mey at Scarfskerry ceased working in 1951 and is now much altered having been converted to residential use. Quite by chance, I met the grandson of the last miller in the village. He recalled running across the fields in his youth to open the sluices, thereby sending the water down to activate the mill-wheel.

Brough is the last small settlement on a neck of land protruding into the Pentland Firth that ends at Dunnet Head. An inspection of the gable in the picture revealed the date AD 1930 (possibly also the date of this photograph), when Brough could claim the most northerly post office on the Scottish mainland. Today the property is known as 'Windhaven', the small post office having gone the way of so many others.

Now the road is surfaced for increased traffic and there is street lighting; then, horses and carts were more usually seen on the unmade road leading to the lighthouse on the headland. Altogether more leisurely days in Brough.

Mill of Mey, Scarfskerry.

The Most Northernly Post Office in Scotland, Brough

Brough Village Dunnet

In 1830 Brough Harbour (above) was a place of immense activity as stone and building materials destined for the new lighthouse under construction on Dunnet Head were landed here. Horses and carts provided onward carriage across the 2½ mile moorland road up to the building site on the headland, the most northerly point of mainland Britain. The renowned builder of lighthouses, Robert Stevenson (grandfather of author RLS), was retained as consulting engineer by the Northern Lighthouse Board, while James Smith of Inverness was the contractor. The erection of light beacons around the Pentland Firth (the first of which was built on the Pentland Skerries in 1794), plus the availability of new charts, proved of great benefit to mariners. Despite standing at a height of 350 feet above sea-level, windows in the tower have been broken by stones hurled up by the waves. The foghorn (extreme right) is no longer used; the crumbling Old Red Sandstone cliffs have caused two earlier ones to fall into the sea. When, in 1989, the staff of three keepers were withdrawn and the light became automatic, a way of life disappeared forever.

DUNNET HEAD FROM THE AIR   BULLETIN PHOTO

The Northern Gate House, built in the early years of the last century for Admiral Sir Alexander Sinclair, gleams white, a conspicuous landmark on Dwarwick Head above Dunnet Bay. A corner window in the drawing room is said to have provided a spyhole through which the Admiral could train his telescope on the sea, providing a sort of crow's-nest view of the 'Northern Gate', as this part of the Pentland Firth is known.

Above and right: The appearance of a photographer along this most distant of coasts about 1905 would have been certain to arouse considerable interest and curiosity. In Dunnet, then as now a small and close-knit community, his visit would have remained a talking-point for some time thereafter.

The village of Dunnet (pictured *c.*1930) is fronted by sand dunes and the spectacular sweep of the bay, while the solid mass of the headland acts as a backdrop. In those days the economy was based on a traditional mix of crofting and fishing, supplemented by income from the occasional tourist seeking accommodation; peat was then commonly used as the source of fuel. The parish church is a mix of several periods, the oldest dating from medieval times; the later tower has a style of construction reminiscent of Canisbay Old Church. The Revd Timothy Pont, a celebrated cartographer who compiled an atlas of Scotland, was the incumbent here early in the seventeenth century. A visitor on holiday attending Sunday church in 1910 noted that the service lasted from 12–2 p.m. and was 'very queer'! (JC)

A horse-drawn coach makes a stop at the Dunnet Hotel *c.*1908 when the village was served by the Thurso, Castletown and Dunnet Head route. In late Victorian times the coach, which left Scarfskerry at 8.30 a.m. bound for Thurso, called here (12 miles, 1¾ hr; fare 1/6d). The hotel is now known as the Northern Sands Hotel.

The origins of the Caithness flagstone industry extend back in time about 370 million years when layers of sediment were progressively laid down in Lake Orcadie, then a vast sea of only modest depth which covered much of Northern Scotland and Orkney. Caithness man has worked the resultant beds of stone since earliest times and acquired both a skill and affinity with this natural resource which is evident in buildings of all types throughout the county down to the present day. The sandstone beds are usually close to surface level, and are layered at 2½° to the

A Caithness Flagstone Quarry

horizontal; removal of the top soil rubble exposes the stone, enabling flags to be raised and extracted using basic tools: wedges, long-handled hammers and five-foot levering poles. Caithness flagstones are a versatile resource, famed for quality and durability. Examples can be seen throughout Scotland and England, even finding their way to London in the Strand and on the concourse of Euston Station. By 1793 the stone was being exported worldwide. Indeed, early Scots emigrants to the New World might have been surprised to discover that the streets of Boston were not, as some suggested, paved with gold, but with flags from Caithness!

Royal Mail at Castletown.

Castletown, once the hub of the industry, prospered from the wealth generated by quarrying. These two scenes show the long, straight Main Street. At Castletown Post Office (now the St Clair Arms Hotel), the Thurso to John O' Groats mail and passenger bus makes a stop sometime before the First World War.

Outside the Commercial Hotel (once a well-known hostelry at the eastern end of the street), groups of onlookers watch the cameraman recording the scene about 1906.

Main Street from East End, Castletown

Wm. Begg, Castletown

Castlehill, Castletown

The Harbour, Castlehill, Castletown.

Castlehill Quarry lies on Dunnet Bay just north of Castletown. The early nineteenth century mansion (top) was the home of James Traill of Rattar, Sheriff of Caithness, who was not only an agricultural improver but also the driving force behind the expansion of the flagstone industry which took place from 1825, the year in which the first cargo was shipped from Castlehill Harbour. This had been built and completed about five years earlier by James Bremner of Keiss. No longer in use, the adjoining quarry now features an interpretative trail where visitors can follow the various processes undergone by the stone from the point of extraction until shipment. Flags were transported to the harbour in horse-drawn trucks pulled along a track before being loaded by hand aboard small schooners. By 1840 over 100 people worked at Castlehill, but at the turn of the twentieth century numbers had increased fivefold. J. T. Calder, the Caithness historian, records that 700–800,000 feet of stone were shipped annually from this small harbour. The quarry fell silent when production ceased in the 1920s, and the 'big house' is no more having burnt down nearly 40 years ago. Today only memories of the past linger on in the quiet corners of Castlehill.

Published by D. Y. Forbes,
Bookseller and Printer, Halkirk

The quarries around Spittal are located south-west of Castletown about nine miles inland as the crow flies, and this is an appropriate place for a final word on the subject as flagstones are still extracted here. In days past the workforce comprised groups of specialists including quarrymen and cutters, while dressers split the stone using double-edged axes. Scuffers removed any blemishes and classers stacked the flags according to size, shape and thickness. Class 1 flags at a thickness of 2½" to 3½" were ideal for paving, while other thicknesses and sizes might be more suitable for alternative uses including roofing ('sheddies') or fencing. Slabs stood on end, embedded in the ground and butted together, make an excellent stock-proof fence, a sight commonly seen in the fields. I met Mr Sutherland at the quarry which bears his name at Spittal, and which has been producing flagstones since 1850. Mechanisation has resulted in fewer men being employed these days, but there remains a steady demand for Caithness stone, which received a particular boost at the Millennium when many new building projects were undertaken country-wide. This picture dates from c.1905.

Georgemas Junction looking south, 1912. A Yankee tank engine is seen taking on water on the Thurso branch line (right), while an Inverness-bound train is held at the signals. This important junction for the Thurso and Wick lines has undergone considerable change since an extensive modernisation programme was implemented in 1989.

Peat Cutters Caithness

The Flow Country is both a complex and fragile environment. Windswept, bleak, largely inaccessible and an almost secret part of Caithness and neighbouring Sutherland, this wilderness of one million acres consists of fast-flowing rivers, lochans, blanket bog and peatland. Other parts produce grain, while elsewhere sheep and cattle are raised in the undulating landscape. Some years ago there were fears that blanket bog might be entirely replaced with blanket forestry, as the rich took advantage of grants and tax breaks to invest heavily in regimented plantations of Lodgepole pines and Sitka spruce which were planted in a landscape that had not seen a tree for more than 6,000 years. Such fears have now receded somewhat. Over the following few pages we will move progressively further into this region of 'Deepest Caithness' which in reality comprises more water than land, and where limited access to a few parts is afforded by the occasional minor road. The Flow Country is traversed by the tracks of the former Highland Railway, and for passengers the scene from the carriage windows is one of unremitting desolation; the remote setting of Altnabreac Station can surely have no equal in Great Britain. Such wetlands are unique in this country and hold the internationally recognised Ramsar designation; they have also been proposed for World Heritage Site status. The area provides a natural habitat for unusual mosses and bog flowers, including insect-devouring butterwort and sundew plants, as well as rare birds such as greenshank, dunlin, golden plover, wood sandpiper and red- and black-throated divers. In short, the Flow Country is outstandingly important and very special.

BRAAL CASTLE

Road signs proclaim Halkirk to be 'Scotland's first planned village'; an equally appropriate claim might also be 'Gateway to the Flow Country'. Two centuries ago, in 1804, Sir John Sinclair of Ulbster commenced building the grid-pattern layout of the settlement beside the Thurso River. The nineteenth century mansion known as Braal Castle – photographed c.1925 and not to be confused with the twelfth century remnants of the principal seat of the Earls of Caithness – was, I understand, occupied by the military during the Second World War and has now been converted into flats.

THE OLD MILL, HALKIRK.

E·4315

Ben Morven Distillery, Halkirk

Published by D. Y. Forbes, Bookseller and Printer, Halkirk

For their respective operations, the Old Mill and the Ben Morven Distillery at Halkirk drew water from the Thurso River on whose banks they stood. Although milling has long ceased, the compact, solid former mill building still stands, while the somewhat rambling (and more modern) distillery located 400 yards from Gerston Farm has vanished. Built in 1886 and known originally as the Gerston Distillery, this second distillery bore the same name as an earlier one which once occupied a nearby site. Sadly, the later distillations were not as popular among high society as the earlier brew, and after a comparatively short life the Ben Morven Distillery closed in 1911 and was progressively dismantled. The tall chimney stack was demolished in 1918, and all the remaining buildings had gone by 1929, with the exception of the still house, which became a dwelling.

Two scenes outside the Ulbster Arms Hotel in Bridge Street, looking north across the bridge.

Top: Built in 1878 the hotel has since expanded and absorbed the business of A. Coutts, no doubt to accommodate the many fishing guests who came and still come here to try their luck on the Thurso River and elsewhere. Once can imagine that the appearance of the Paisley-built Arrol–Johnston car in the village must have generated some excitement, for the date of the picture was certainly before 8 October 1906, as confirmed by the post office cancellation on this postcard mailed from Thurso.

Above: D. Y. Forbes, the publisher of this postcard, produced some excellent local cards as well as a *Photographic View Album of Halkirk* almost a century ago. Forbes' well-known business in Bridge Street stood only a few yards from where this photograph was taken. His shop, although somewhat structurally altered, still stands today and his name remains over the door – a link with the past.

✺ D. Y. FORBES, ✺

BOOKSELLER, STATIONER, PRINTER, and NEWSAGENT,
BRIDGE STREET, HALKIRK,

BEGS TO DRAW ATTENTION TO THE FOLLOWING LINES:

PRINTING

EXECUTED ON THE PREMISES.

Notepaper Headings.
Visiting Cards.
Invitations and
Wedding Cards.
Cake Cards.
Accounts and Memos.
'In Memoriam' Cards.
&c., &c. ...

—◈—

PRINTING IN GOLD, SILVER, AND
COLOURS.

MAGAZINES, PERIODICALS,
DAILY AND WEEKLY
NEWSPAPERS.

——

CIGARS, CIGARETTES,
TOBACCO,
AND SMOKERS' REQUISITES.

——

PAPERHANGINGS.
Large Stock—Choice Designs.

——

PICTURE FRAMING
In Latest Mouldings.

——

FISHING RODS AND TACKLE.

——

Agent for
EDISON BELL PHONOGRAPH.

Immense Range of
Photo and other Frames,
in Latest Patterns.

—◈—

Photo Albums,
Hand Bags, Purses,
Gladstone & Brief Bags,
Cutlery and
Electro-Plate.
Fountain Pens.
Spectacles.

—◈—

STATIONERY
Of every Description, at Keenest
Prices.

Advertisement from the *Photographic View Album of Halkirk, c.*1910.

'The Halkirk Express', another gem of a postcard published by D. Y. Forbes, was mailed from the local post office in July 1908. The sender asks 'What do you think of our motor which brings the mail?' I believe this unusual conveyance, seemingly an adapted handcart, not only undertook local deliveries but also transported the incoming and outgoing mail for the village to and from Halkirk Station on the Highland Railway line. Unfortunately, at the time of publication, further details have proved elusive.

Millicent, Duchess of Sutherland, is shown leaving the Ross Institute Bazaar. The general untidiness of the scene and incomplete state of the surroundings on the Bridge Street frontage indicate that this is an early photograph of the Institute, probably dating from 1912. The gate piers and walls surmounted by light holders and iron railings had yet to make an appearance (see below).

Designed by architect Sinclair Macdonald and gifted to the community by local resident John Ross, Halkirk's cultural centre, the Ross Institute, is dignified and impressive both by design and scale. The clock was donated by another resident, David Murray, and is claimed to be the first electric clock incorporated in any Scottish public building. The fact that Alexander Bain, the inventor of the electric clock, was born in neighbouring Watton, surely makes this something of an historic double first for Caithness.

Right: Bridge Street looking south *c.*1910. In those days to see children barefoot between May and September was not unusual.

Centre and below: Halkirk level crossing and the adjoining railway station, about 1930. Either side of Halkirk, Scotrail trains (following the route of what was formerly the Highland Railway) still make stops at Scotscalder and Georgemas Junction, but not so here where the station closed in 1960. Nowadays, scant evidence survives that a station ever existed.

LEVEL CROSSING, HALKIRK.

E.43/8.

THE STATION, HALKIRK.

Westerdale, a scattering of houses four miles south of Halkirk, is reached by a minor road which passes the local 'big house' (Dale House) and close to the formerly significant (but now disused) Westerdale Mill, which stands by the old bridge over the Thurso River. Beyond Westerdale, thoughts of having left behind the last outpost of civilisation spring to mind as the road continues deeper into the Flow Country towards Strathmore

Strathmore Lodge,   Halkirk.

Lodge, three miles distant. With not a human habitation in sight, the loneliness of the surroundings is apparent at every turn as one becomes increasingly enveloped in this huge landscape so typical of the flowlands. Eventually the lodge – the first of a cluster of fishing and sporting lodges claimed by some to be the finest in Caithness – comes into view, but surprisingly is much smaller than shown in this *c.*1900 view. A serious fire gutted roughly half of Strathmore Lodge (the right-hand portion), which was later demolished.

Loch More receives a great volume of water from a vast catchment area, and this is carried the length of the Thurso River to the sea. In times of even modest rainfall, perhaps occurring many miles away, the water level in the loch can rise quickly and alarmingly to spill over the barrage shown here and thunder down the fish ladder adjoining Lochmore Cottage. That this former estate worker's dwelling still stands is a marvel, for its two rooms have been inundated in the past. To have been living here when the water was in full spate, especially at night, must have been a terrifying experience, for no help would have been at hand. Nowadays the cottage acts as a base for salmon fishermen, and inside, as we raised our voices above the roar of water only feet away, one told me about the fishing, explaining that the construction of the dam and ladder had been undertaken by P. D. Malloch of Perth about 1907. Loch More is also noted for its pink-fleshed trout: here in the summer of 1908 two rods got a basket of 353 trout in the course of a day and a half.

This page depicts three more fishing and sporting lodges off the beaten track in the Flow Country.

I was assured that this story told me in Halkirk was true. Years ago a telegraph boy from Halkirk Post Office had pedalled to Dalnawillan Lodge *twice* in one day bearing telegrams announcing the birth of a son to Lord Thurso – a distance there and back of 28 miles each time!

Dalnawillan Lodge, Altnabreac

Glutt Lodge Altnabreac

'I have put a cross over the house. The other buildings are the garage, the keeper's house, dairy, cowsheds, the men's and girls' rooms and kennels. Major Graves has some very fine sporting dogs. We call it our world on our own; I would rather be in heaven sleeping with the angels. You notice there are no trees or flowers.' This postcard was written from Glutt Lodge in 'Deepest Caithness' before the First World War. The buildings are much changed today.

Lochdhu Lodge, built in 1895 for Lord Thurso, is another isolated outpost which remained in family ownership for about 85 years, seeing service as a hotel in its final phase. The lodge, which comprises some 45 rooms, once played host to Sir Winston Churchill, but what he thought of the lurid wavy-lined pattern of coloured roof slates history does not record. In August 1909 'Dora' wrote that 'while we arrived safely, it seemed an endless time coming and is very lonely'.

Altnabreac Station, Caithnessshire.

The fledgling, cash-strapped railway companies pushing their lines north and west of Inverness in Victorian times were often held to ransom by landowners – who were also sometimes railway directors – demanding a price for allowing the iron road across their estates. Frequently that price included the provision of a station solely for their use. A mile north-west of Lochdhu Lodge is Altnabreac Station, a solitary railway outpost in the middle of nowhere. As in some other instances along the line, the siting of such a station would prove useful for transporting building materials for the nearby lodge under construction in the 1890s. In the early years of the twentieth century a mere scattering of people supported a tiny school and a post office which stamped mail with the Altnabreac postmark. Today, the station – downgraded to a request stop – is much changed from this photograph of *c*.1907, and serves only the occasional passenger, very likely to be a fishing or shooting guest at one of the lodges. The sense of total isolation felt in this part of the Flow Country a century ago is emphasised by just five words put on this postcard by the same hand that wrote the message from Glutt Lodge: 'This is our only hope'!

On the desolate, bleak moors wind-borne snow can quickly drift to house height, and not for nothing did Victorian railwaymen refer to Caithness as 'The County of Snow Drifts'. Reproduced from a postcard captioned 'Entombed in a snow drift near Thurso', this photograph could in reality have been taken anywhere between Forsinard in Sutherland and Wick.

Heavy snow has always been a very real hazard to the operation of the railway in this part of Scotland. Even in comparatively recent years, trains bound for Caithness have been stranded in snow, requiring passengers to be rescued from the Borrobol Estate in Strath Halladale, while another train was missing for several hours before being found in huge drifts beyond the county march east of Forsinard. During the appalling winter of 1894/5 a fish train from Wick bound for the southern markets became trapped and buried in a raging blizzard at the Fairy Hillocks at Altnabreac causing the crew to abandon her. Subsequently, after ten days of digging, the consignment was released from the natural deep-freeze and the herring were found to be in perfect condition. These photographs show the two ways of attacking the drifts. Digging out required gangs of workmen wielding shovels and was long, hard and laborious work. (JGH) The alternative was more dramatic, as three steam engines linked together and fronted by a snowplough charged the drifts at 60 mph, producing a spectacular sight and sound, as here at Scotscalder in 1909. (JC)

A Caithness Farm Scene.

From the Flow Country a return to the coast is made via Halkirk to Thurso East, five miles west of Castletown. The castellated mansion built in the 1870s by Sir Tollemache Sinclair replaced an earlier building of 1660. His Thurso Castle (pictured below *c.*1910) had a magnificent setting looking over the sea: the statuary, well-manicured lawns and sheltered tennis court all combined to exude an aura of wealth and power so typical of a laird's house in the Victorian age. But that was all long ago, and a reversal of fortunes saw the mansion finally abandoned and largely demolished in 1952 so that only birds now reside among the ruins, whose loftier parts point starkly skywards like broken teeth. In the early twentieth century, Sir Archibald Sinclair, 1st Viscount Thurso, owned almost a quarter of the county's 439,000 acres, but following his death in 1970 the family's estate has contracted in size very considerably. His son, Robin Macdonald Sinclair, inherited not only a strong political tradition but also an estate which proved financially unviable. He died in 1995 and will be remembered particularly as the founder and first chairman of Caithness Glass, and for his work as President of the Boys' Brigade – most appropriate, for Thurso was the birthplace of Sir William Smith, founder of that organisation.

THURSO CASTLE

The Thurso River is the king of Caithness rivers. The first *Statistical Account of Scotland* notes that 2,560 salmon were taken from the river in one day in 1736, while in 1926 the yield was 2,240, the highest individual weight being a fish of 47 lbs. These photographs at the mouth of the river show two very different harvests, this time from the sea – one comparatively small, the other very large indeed.

JOHN O' GROAT SERIES   CAIRNIE, CHEMIST, THURSO

A REMARKABLE CAPTURE OF WHALES WAS MADE AT THURSO ON THE PENTLAND FIRTH ON JUNE 19TH 1899. HALF-A-DOZEN FISHING BOATS FOUGHT THEM FROM NOON TILL SIX O'CLOCK BEFORE THEY WERE DRIVEN INTO SHALLOW WATER AND SPEARED.   THE SCHOOL NUMBERED 104.

To the Viking invaders, Thurso must have had a certain importance as they bestowed the name *Thor's-a* – literally the river of the god Thor – on the settlement. The height of their power was reached in the eleventh century under Thorfinn who defeated the army of King Duncan's nephew at Thurso in AD 1040. Created a burgh in 1633, Thurso has historically been the commercial centre of the north coast and once had a thriving import and export trade conducted with the ports of Scandinavia, the Baltic and the Low Countries. In fact, by the fourteenth century, Thurso had become such an important trading centre that the weights used in the town were made the standard for the whole of Scotland. Exports included a variety of agricultural produce, fish and, until the 1920s, Caithness flagstones. *Above:* A view of the fishing quarter from Thurso Castle. (JC) *Below:* In 1901 the town's population was 3,930. Moored sailing vessels are seen against the background of Old St Peter's Church, kippering sheds and fishermen's houses. The quays which once bustled with activity are now silent and the trading vessels so commonly seen in years past have vanished.

Thurso Harbour

Despite the many changes wrought by the twentieth century, a sense of antiquity still pervades the narrow streets and lanes in parts of Old Thurso where the name of Rotterdam Street brings to mind the town's entrepôt trade in days of sail. The Turnpike in Shore Street (pictured in 1919) is believed to have been a seventeenth century merchant's house. One of the celebrities in the old quarter was Robert Dick (1811–66), a local baker now remembered as a renowned geologist and botanist. The rocks, mountains and moorlands of Caithness were as familiar to him as the oven of his own bakehouse, and his collection of botanical specimens ('the herbarium') has been carefully preserved for posterity. Among his achievements was the identification of the northern holy grass, common in Norway, but growing only in Scotland on the banks of the Thurso River.

Near the riverside, the architectural jewel of Old Thurso is the ruined St Peter's Church, which authorities believe was founded c.1220 by Gilbert Murray, Bishop of Caithness. The fabric consists of work undertaken during several different periods in history, and there is much surviving detail of interest including the Gothic traceried windows and old tombstones in the churchyard. The boy sitting on the tomb in the foreground in 1919 was airbrushed from the scene in later editions of this postcard, possibly as the pose was thought disrespectful. In 1832 the church closed for worship when services transferred to the new church of St Peter and St Andrew in Princes Street.

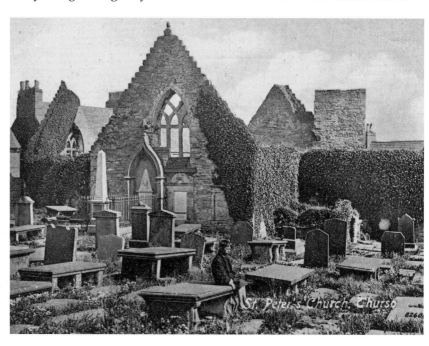

The combination of High Street (above), which links Rotterdam Street and Shore Street, forms the main thoroughfare of the old town. These pictures from a century ago illustrate the Gothic town hall of 1870 (top) and an interesting street scene showing a good deal of activity where Market Street and Couper Street bisect High Street from left to right. The former, of course, recalls earlier days when one of the town's principal markets was held there. Here, too, there have been changes, one of these being the removal of the monument in the roadway (left). The fountain, dated 1898 and in memory of Dr John Grant Smith (Thurso's physician for 44 years), has been relocated and can now be found on the greensward of the Esplanade overlooking the bay.

St Andrew's Free Church in Olrig Street (top) opened in 1871, replacing the former Free Church nearby which had been built immediately following the Disruption of 1843. Apparently that place of worship had a certain reputation for drowsiness, as one visitor noted that during a service he saw 600 people asleep! Perhaps in those days there was some excuse as many had walked considerable distances, and to say that sermons then were lengthy would be an understatement. Sadly, the elegant St Andrew's, built in Gothic style, is no longer in use as a church and many of the interior fittings have been removed.

THURSO FROM THE AIR   BULLETIN PHOTO

Thurso has undergone three clearly defined phases of expansion which can be traced through its architecture: in the seventeenth and eighteenth centuries around the harbour (out of view to the right in this photograph); from 1800 in the Georgian new town (shown here) laid out by Sir John Sinclair of Ulbster; and latterly since the 1950s in the peripheral development necessitated by the influx of technicians for the Dounreay project, which caused the population to triple within a decade. The regular grid pattern of broad streets is well illustrated by this aerial photograph taken *c.*1930 above the bridge over the Thurso River. The road leads directly into the new town where St Peter's and St Andrew's Church can be seen in Princes Street. To the left of the bridge are the substantial riverside villas of Janet Street whose gardens and old stables back on to Brabster Street; beyond lie the main thoroughfares of Sinclair Street, Traill Street and Princes Street, while to the right Olrig Street leads away past St Andrew's Free Church through countryside (then devoid of development) towards Scrabster. Sharp-eyed residents will note much of interest in this picture of Thurso's Georgian quarter, which some consider a worthy northern parallel to Edinburgh's New Town.

Quieter days in Sir George's Street, looking up from the bridge towards Traill Street and the church of St Peter and St Andrew in Princes Street beyond. The house with a cross incised on the wall stands at the junction with Janet Street, while opposite, the tower of the Episcopal Church is visible. Freed of today's traffic, this scene from an earlier age has a timeless quality.

Above: Traill Street (seen here *c*.1914) continues into Sinclair Street, at the end of which is the Miller Institution in Davidson's Lane. The imposing, classical building – originally a school and now the public library – is surmounted by a domed clock tower and was gifted to the town by the Revd Alexander Miller DD of Buckie in 1862. *Below:* In this late 1930s view looking towards Rotterdam Street in the old quarter, road signs abound to assist the motorist, emphasising the importance of Traill Street as the principal thoroughfare. AA and RAC emblems are displayed over the entrance to the Royal Hotel.

In a travel guide of 1884, the Royal Hotel is classed as 'good and highly spoken of', while exactly 50 years later an advertisement claims 'One of the finest hotels in Scotland. Conveniently situated for the Orkney Isles. One hundred bedrooms with running hot and cold water. Garage for 50 cars. Excellent trout fishing on all best Caithness lochs.' At that time the proprietor, James Wilson, had three other hotels in his charge – Ormlie Lodge (Thurso), the Golf Links Hotel (Dunnet) and the Forsinard Hotel in Sutherland. The Royal is pictured here c.1905.

Mansons Lane, off Traill Street, takes its name from Alex Manson who established a brewery there in the late eighteenth century. For centuries the little circular building known as the Meadow Well housed the town's main water supply. Capacity was increased in 1818, and the present pump, installed about 1850, remained in use until the 1920s to fill water carts damping down the dusty streets. However, more than a source of water, the Meadow Well was also a meeting place where townsfolk would chat and exchange news.

Above: The assassination of a little-known archduke in an obscure Balkans town during the summer of 1914 sparked a chain of events which unfolded with bewildering speed to plunge Europe into war. August 14 saw a large contingent of bluejackets passing through Thurso Station and along Princes Street en route to Scrabster, bound for the Orkney naval base at Scapa Flow. The extent of casualties in the First World War proved to be on a horrifying and hitherto unimagined scale, resulting in what historians refer to as the 'lost generation'. For many of the men seen here, these would be their final hours on British soil, as large numbers were destined never to see their native shores again.

Centre: Victoria Walk, an extension of the Esplanade built in 1882 linking the town to the Scrabster road, provides fine views of Thurso Bay. Note the use of Caithness flags as boundary markers here (*c.*1903) and in the lower picture.

Below: While the present 'big house' has stood on the skyline above Scrabster and the bay for the past 170 years, no one can say when the site was occupied originally. Subsequent residential development has left Scrabster House in splendid isolation no longer.

The early mail services for Orkney and Shetland were routed north of Wick via Huna, near John O' Groats. Almost unbelievably the mails were taken onward by a six-oared open boat which was rowed eight miles across the Pentland Firth and landed on an exposed shore at Burwick (South Ronaldsay). Scrabster's port developed from the 1850s, achieving added status when the mailboat service to Stromness was introduced in 1856. To this day strong links are maintained with Orkney. The bustling port, almost unrecognisable from this photograph, has seen much expansion in recent years, and the building of the oil terminal, a project which received the support of the late Lord Thurso, has provided an additional dimension. Holborn Head lighthouse can be seen on the point.

The new lifeboat house, 1906. Fifty years later (on 18 August 1956 to be precise) the late Queen Mother officially named Thurso's new lifeboat *Dunnet Head*. Donated by the Civil Service Lifeboat Fund at a cost of £35,000, she was one of the latest and most up-to-date vessels then in service. However, just four months after the naming ceremony both lifeboat and shed, together with launching gear, winch and workshop, were entirely destroyed in a disastrous fire.

Right and centre: The migratory herring brought Scrabster alive during the season, producing scenes which have become familiar in this book, although the sheer scale of the activity never ceases to amaze. Scrabster House dominates the skyline in the first of these two scenes from the early 1890s.

Below: The changing face of Scrabster: a scene from the past as fisher girls gut and pack herring in front of West End House. Today, the windows of the house take in a close-up view of the oil terminal.

SCRABSTER IN THE HERRING SEASON.   B.4696.

Problems of access from the harbour took four years to resolve before those renowned lighthouse engineers, the Stevensons, could build their light at Holborn Head in 1862. The particularly fine photograph at the top of this page looks down on ships lying in Scrabster Roads c.1910. On the headland nearby are two outstanding examples of coastal erosion: the Deil's Brig (a natural rock bridge), and Clett Rock, a detached stack rising some 150 feet from the sea, which is crowned with large numbers of seabirds during the breeding season.

Five miles west of Thurso, a diversion from the main road followed by a three-quarter mile walk across a headland finds the twelfth century ruins of St Mary's Chapel above Crosskirk Bay. This, one of the oldest ecclesiastical buildings in Caithness, was a chapel subordinate to neighbouring Reay, where the existence of a ninth century gravestone in the churchyard suggests the latter was once a place of even greater religious significance. St Mary's is well worth a visit, although the towering wind turbine nearby does not sit easily with the ancient monument.

At Forss there are trees – something for which Caithness is not renowned. Crows drift lazily on the wind above woods surrounding the 'big house' around which the Forss Water winds on three sides on its way to the sea. Forss House, a substantial M-gabled mansion crowned with distinctive chimney stacks, has stood here for 200 years and is now a country house hotel. One of the more exotic previous owners was Major Radclyffe, an enthusiastic big game hunter and fisherman, whose initials appear with the date 1939 on the porch above the entrance. That was the year he removed the existing porch shown in this photograph, adding a much larger one which became his trophy room. This he filled with animal heads, skins and mounted specimens shot or hooked during his forays around the world.

The Forss Water is a fine salmon river, and if proof were needed there is an excellent mounted specimen of 42 lbs, having a length of 46" and girth of 25½", exhibited in the bar at the house. The waters make an impressive sight, especially in spate, as they thunder across the falls between former meal mills either side of the river (seen here *c.*1900). One has been converted into residential use while the other remains derelict. The fact that the river formed a boundary between two grain-growing parishes gave each the opportunity for a riverside mill. A redundant circular millstone lies in view of the entrance to Forss House, while two others I was told had been acquired by Golspie Mill in Sutherland. Beside a path within sight of the falls, a stone tablet records that the ashes of Major and Mrs Radclyffe of Forss House had been interred there on ground consecrated in 1972. In all probability the Major is still fishing somewhere in the Great Beyond.

My knowledge of the intricacies surrounding the nuclear power industry is somewhat less than superficial, but I recall a thought-provoking sub-headline in *The Times* more than 35 years ago: 'Expansion in Reduction Plant at Dounreay'. Over a period of 50 years the facility at Dounreay has grown to employ some 2,000 personnel, becoming the biggest single employer in Caithness and bringing huge financial benefit to the local economy. However, opponents of the industry would, no doubt, wish to highlight a less happy aspect in that notices all along the shore at nearby Sandside warn of the presence of radioactive particles. Those interested should visit the exhibition. This photograph by John Adams, captioned 'Dounreay Experimental Atomic Reactor Establishment', shows what was, in the early 1950s, a very startlingly shaped – even futuristic – building.

West of Forss, the road into Sutherland is never far from the sea. Before degenerating into bare moorland at Drumholliston, the route traverses Reay – a landscape dotted with neat farmsteads which supported a scattered population of 719 in 1931. The parish has been home to Clan Mackay for centuries, and the old clan lands once stretched away into Sutherland. Indeed, the whole area is still known as 'the Mackay country'. This is Reay c.1930: the post office (centre), parish church, and (left) the war memorial and old inn. In 1885 the horse-drawn mail coach left Thurso at 7 a.m. calling at several inns along the route including Reay (fare 1/6d), eventually arriving at Tongue, the 46 mile journey taking 9 hours (fare 7/6d). The minister of Reay, the Revd Alexander Pope, deserves a mention, for it was he who in the 1730s rode his pony all the way to Twickenham – *and back* – to meet his namesake, the poet Alexander Pope. A friendship resulted from this incredible pilgrimage and the two Alexanders subsequently exchanged correspondence, thus maintaining the unlikeliest of links between Twickenham and this remote parish.

Sandside Bay has been settled since earliest times, and both Pictish and Viking settlements, along with the old village of Reay, are said to lie buried under the sand dunes. The harbour was built in 1830 by James Bremner for Major William Innes of Sandside House, and a particular aspect of the construction, well-illustrated by this 1930s photograph, is the superb masonry work which includes the innovative feature of vertical courses of rough-hewn stone to combat wave impact. Cod and saithe were the mainstay of the early nineteenth century fishery, later supplemented seasonally by herring.

Sandside House is the last Caithness 'big house' along this coast. The pointers photographed in 1904 against the gamekeeper's peat stack on the estate make an unusual picture. This postcard was franked at Reay Post Office on 26 December that year, and at Thurso the same day; not even Boxing Day was allowed to delay the progress of His Majesty's postal service.

The hill of Drumholliston is in reality a stretch of wild moorland extending several miles and straddling the county boundary between Caithness and Sutherland. The moor is fully exposed to the northern elements, a bleak and desolate terrain, especially in winter, and in an earlier age when there was no road, travellers on foot or horseback viewed a crossing with a degree of apprehension, and with good reason. The boggy tracks were treacherous by day, while a night-time journey was an experience few would undertake willingly. Fisherfolk returning home to the west coast on foot carrying their accumulated seasonal earnings from the Caithness fishing ports had to pass this way; those unwise enough to venture alone on to the moor in darkness would have to run the gauntlet of robbers and vagabonds intent on relieving them of their gold. The boulder known as the Split Stone of Drumholliston formerly marked the county boundary and, according to some tales, was split by the Devil himself. Over the years, stories of the supernatural and of unexplained ghostly happenings all combined to give Drumholliston a fearsome reputation. Standing by the great boulder and looking back to Caithness for the last time, I doubted whether today's travellers speeding along the modern highway spared a thought for either the moor or the stone. Ahead lies the Halladale Bridge and Melvich; Sutherland, the 'Land of Mountains', beckons.